SELFISH PIGS

ANDY RILEY IS THE AUTHOR/ARTIST OF :

THE BOOK OF BUNNY SUICIDES, RETURN OF THE BUNNY SUICIDES, GREAT LIES TO TELL SMALL KIDS, LOADS MORE LIES TO TELL SMALL KIDS, THE BUMPER BOOK OF BUNNY SUICIDES AND D.I.Y. DENTISTRY (AND OTHER ALARMING INVENTIONS). HIS WEEKLY CARTOON STRIP, ROASTED, RUNS IN THE OBSERVER MAGAZINE AND IS ALSO COMPILED AS A HODDER & STOUGHTON HARDBACK.

HIS SCRIPTWRITING WORK INCLUDES BLACK BOOKS, HYPERDRIVE, LITTLE BRITAIN, THE ARMSTRONG AND MILLER SHOW, SMACK THE PONY, THE ARMANDO IANNUCCI SHOWS, SO GRAHAM NORTON, THE 99p CHALLENGE, SLACKER CATS, SPITTING IMAGE, KATY BRAND'S BIG ASS SHOW, THE FRIDAY NIGHT ARMISTICE, AND THE BAFTA-WINNING ANIMATION ROBBIE THE REINDEER.

LOOK OUT FOR NEW CARTOONS AT:

misterandyriley.com

ON TWITTER:

@ andyrileyish

SELFISH PIGS

WHAT?

ANDY RILEY

H
HODDER &
STOUGHTON

FIRST PUBLISHED IN GREAT BRITAIN IN 2009 BY HODDER & STOUGHTON, A HACHETTE UK COMPANY

3 5 7 9 10 8 6 4 2

COPYRIGHT © ANDY RILEY 2009

A CIP CATALOGUE RECORD FOR THIS TITLE IS AVAILABLE FROM THE BRITISH LIBRARY

ISBN HOME 978 0 340 92028 2
ISBN EXPORT 978 0 340 91971 2

PRINTED AND BOUND BY WILLIAM CLOWES LIMITED

HODDER & STOUGHTON POLICY IS TO USE PAPERS THAT ARE NATURAL, RENEWABLE AND RECYCLABLE PRODUCTS AND MADE FROM WOOD GROWN IN SUSTAINABLE FORESTS. THE LOGGING AND MANUFACTURING PROCESSES ARE EXPECTED TO CONFORM TO THE ENVIRONMENTAL REGULATIONS OF THE COUNTRY OF ORIGIN.

HODDER & STOUGHTON LTD.
338 EUSTON ROAD
LONDON NW1 3BH
WWW. HODDER . CO. UK

WITH THANKS TO:

BEN DUNN, CAMILLA HORNBY,
JACK FOGG, KEVIN CECIL,
POLLY FABER, KATIE DAVISON,
ALL AT HODDER & STOUGHTON

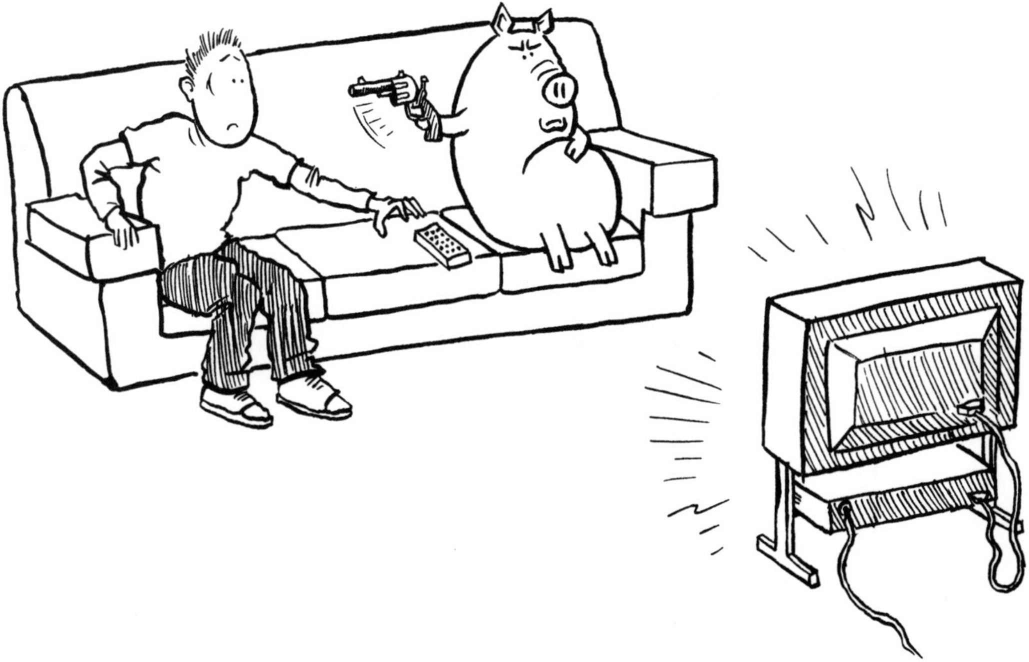

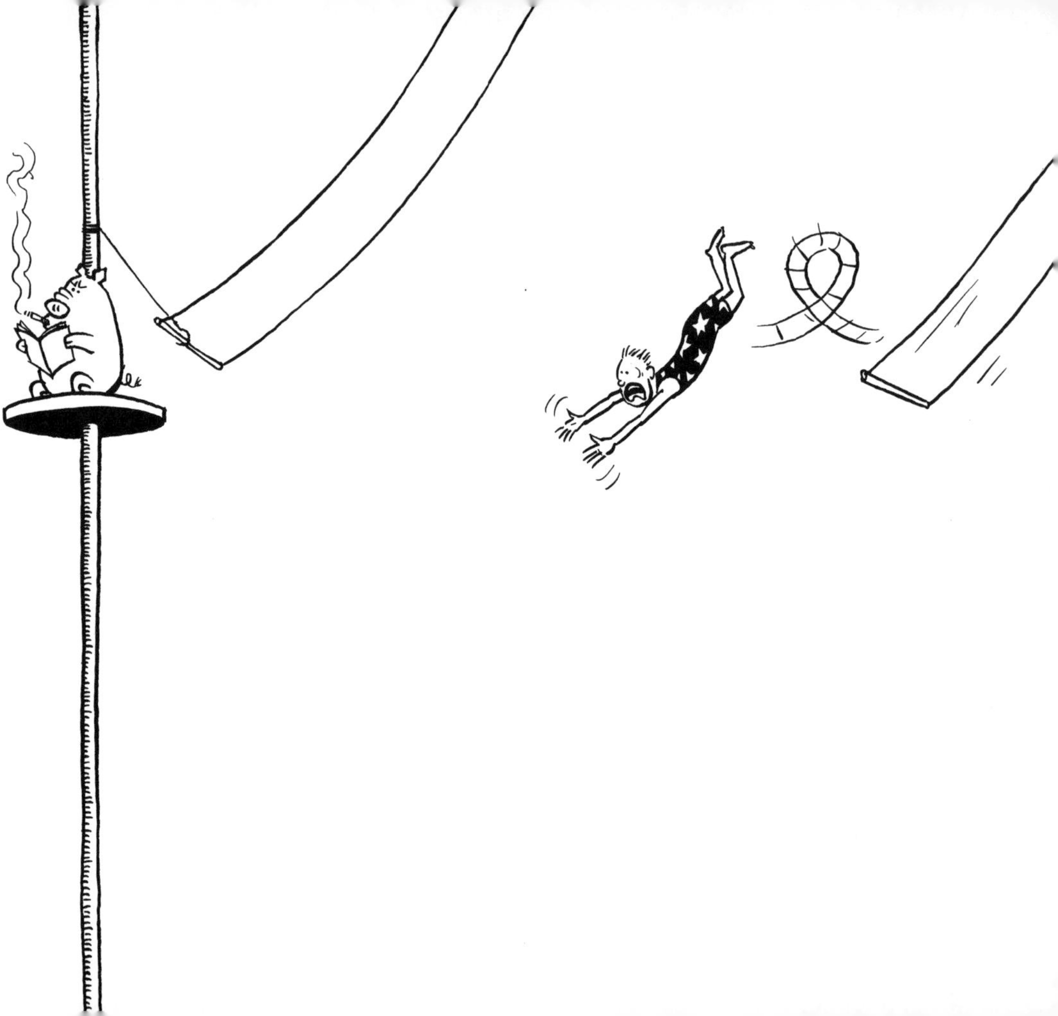

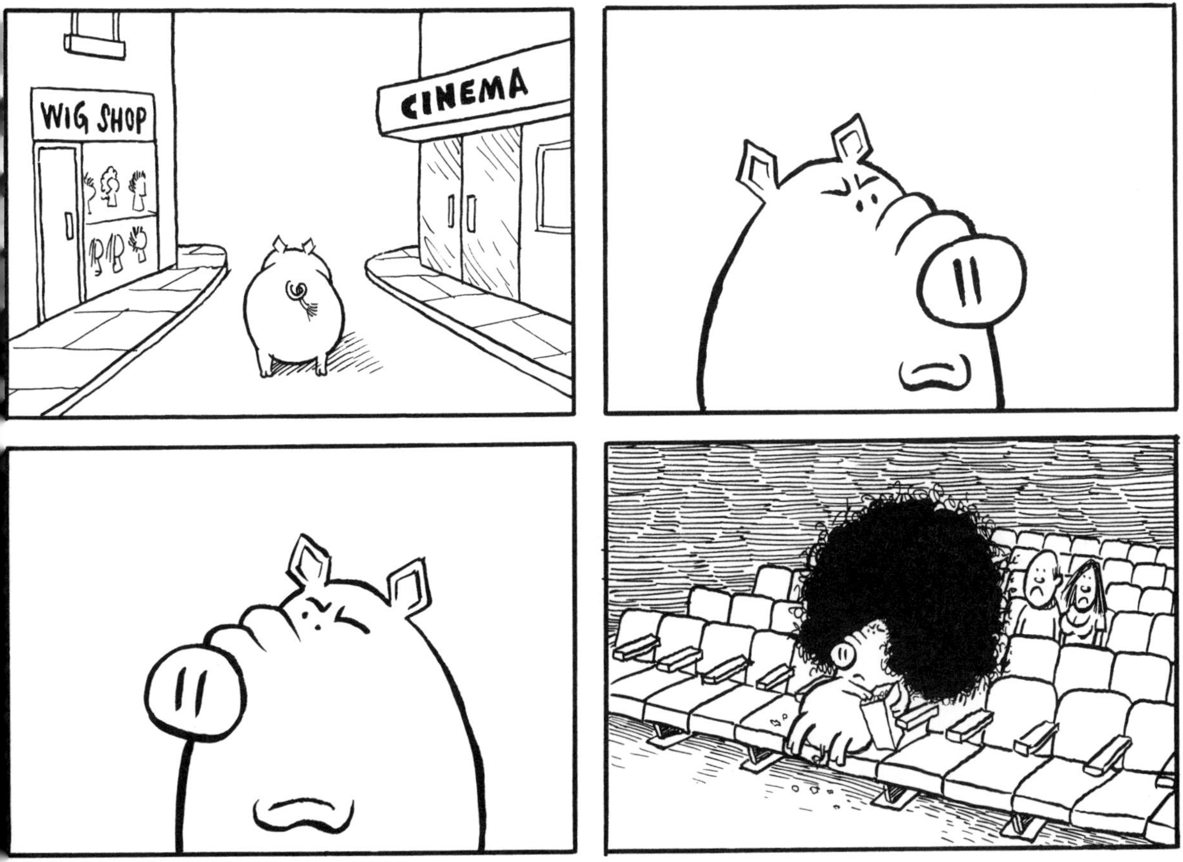
WIG SHOP
CINEMA

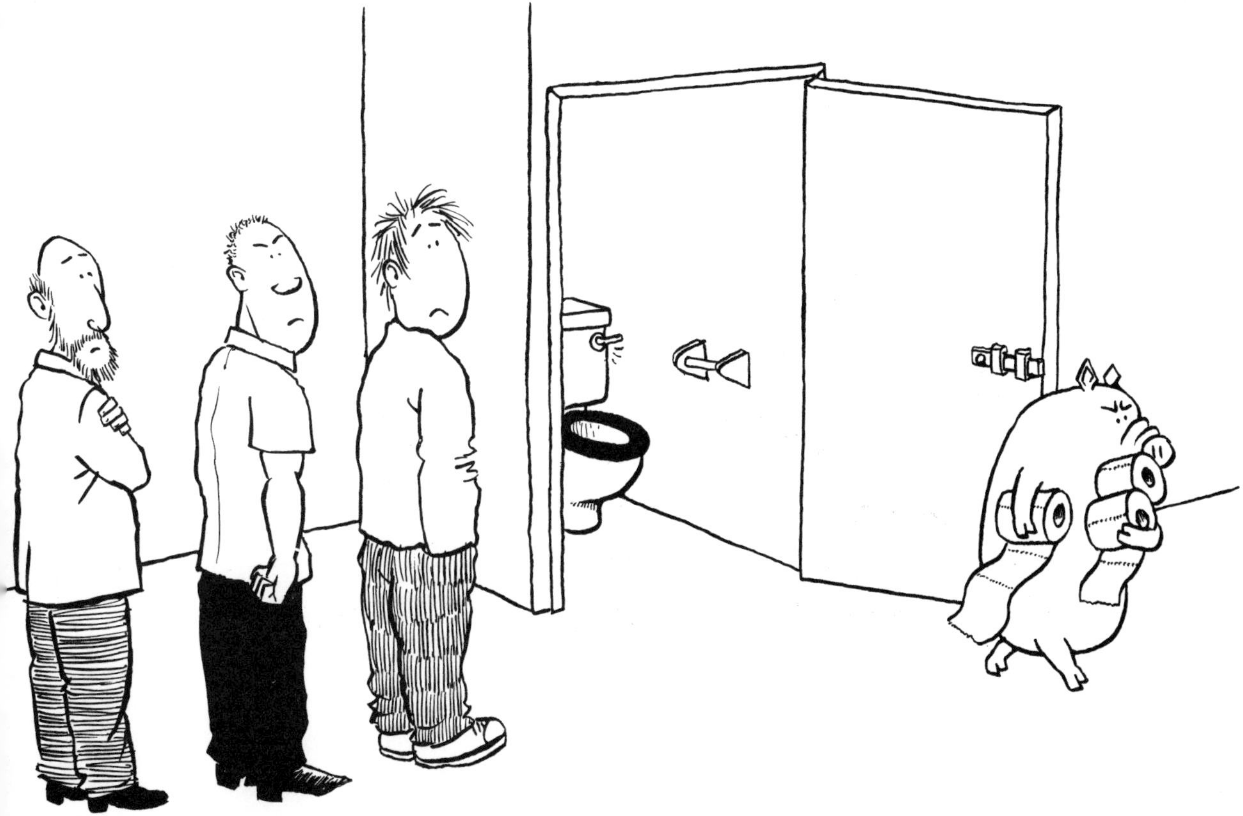

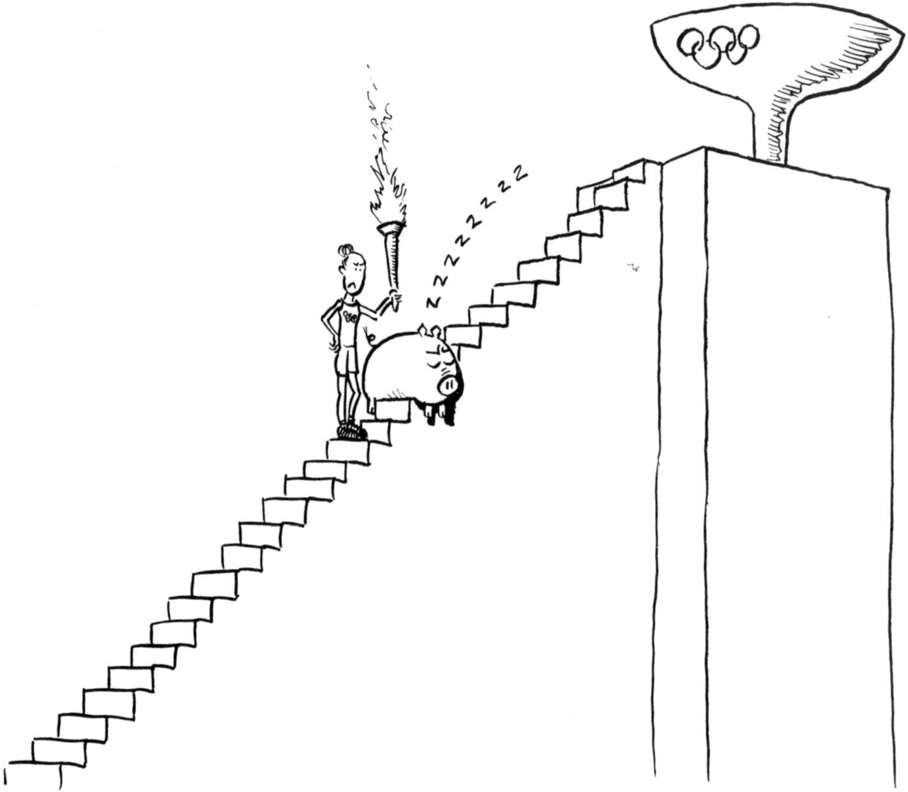
ZZZZZZZZ

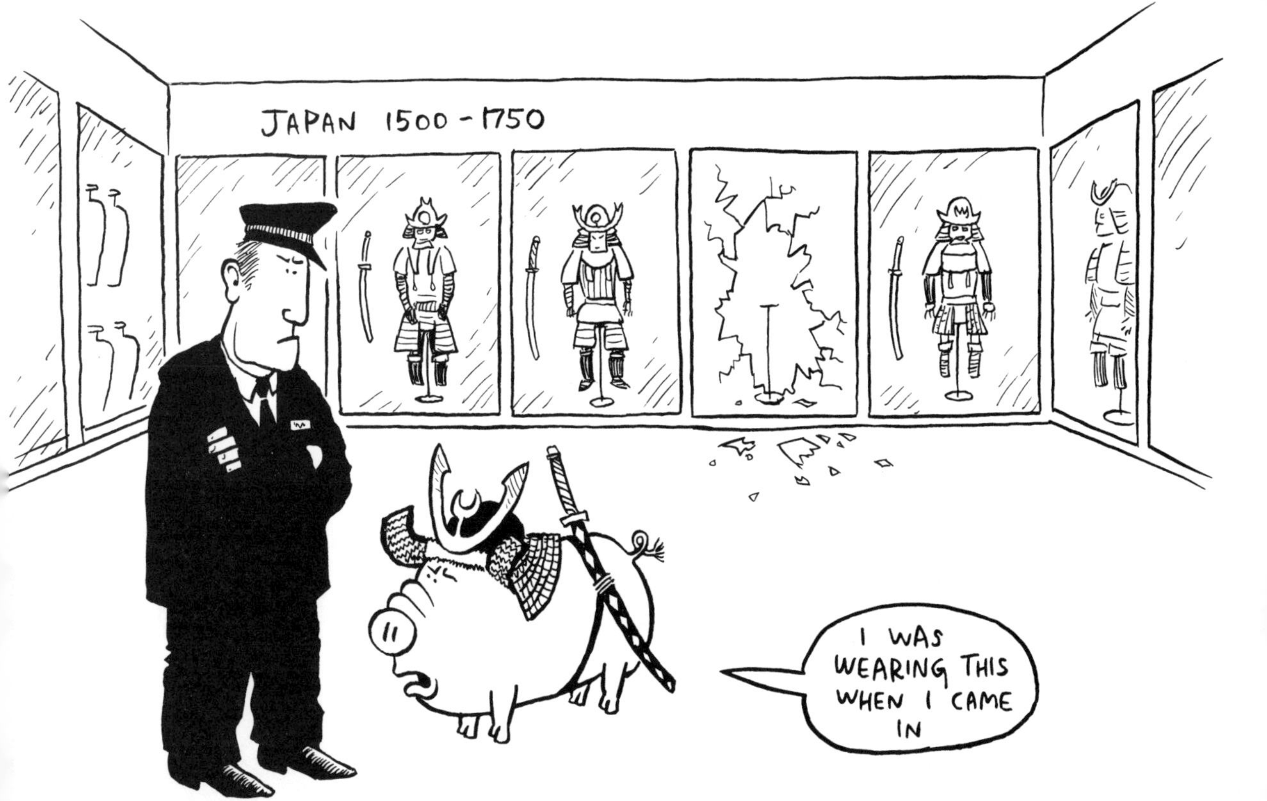
JAPAN 1500 - 1750
I WAS WEARING THIS WHEN I CAME IN

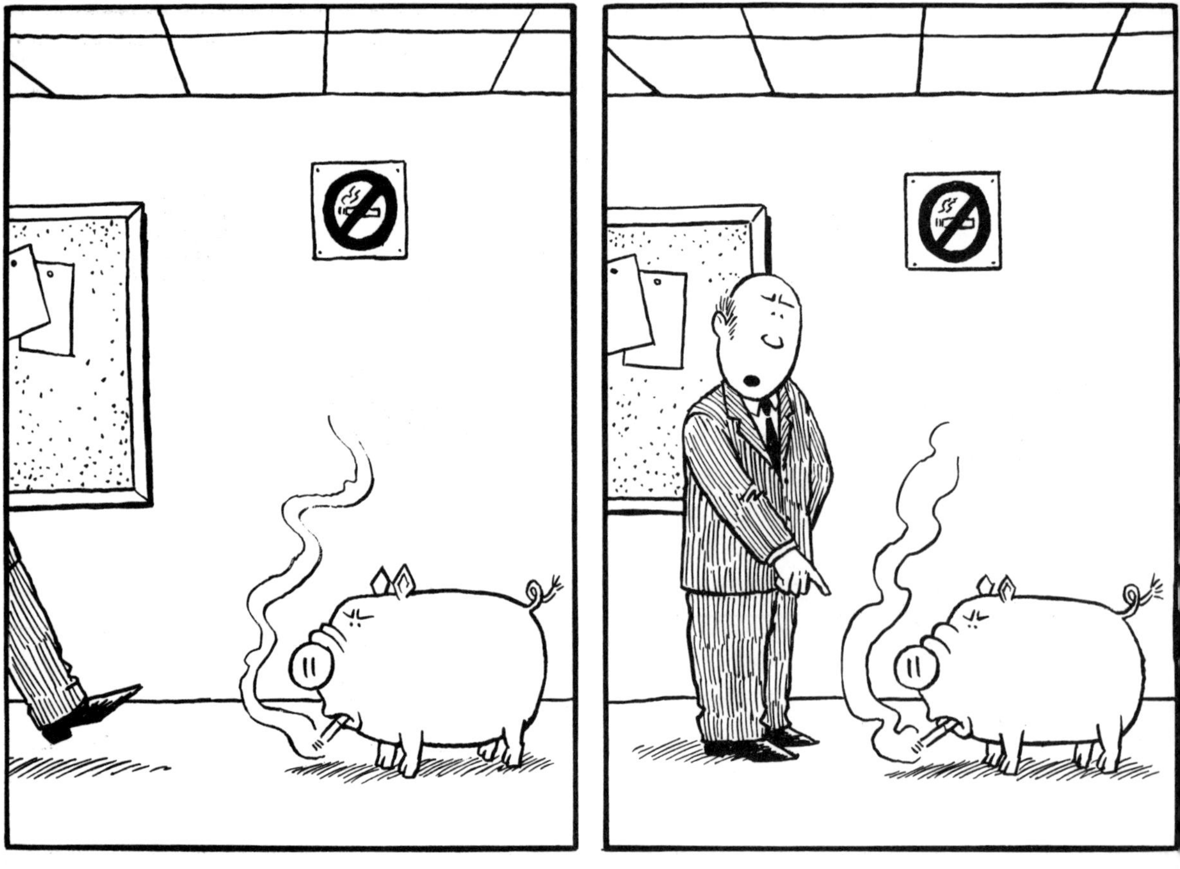

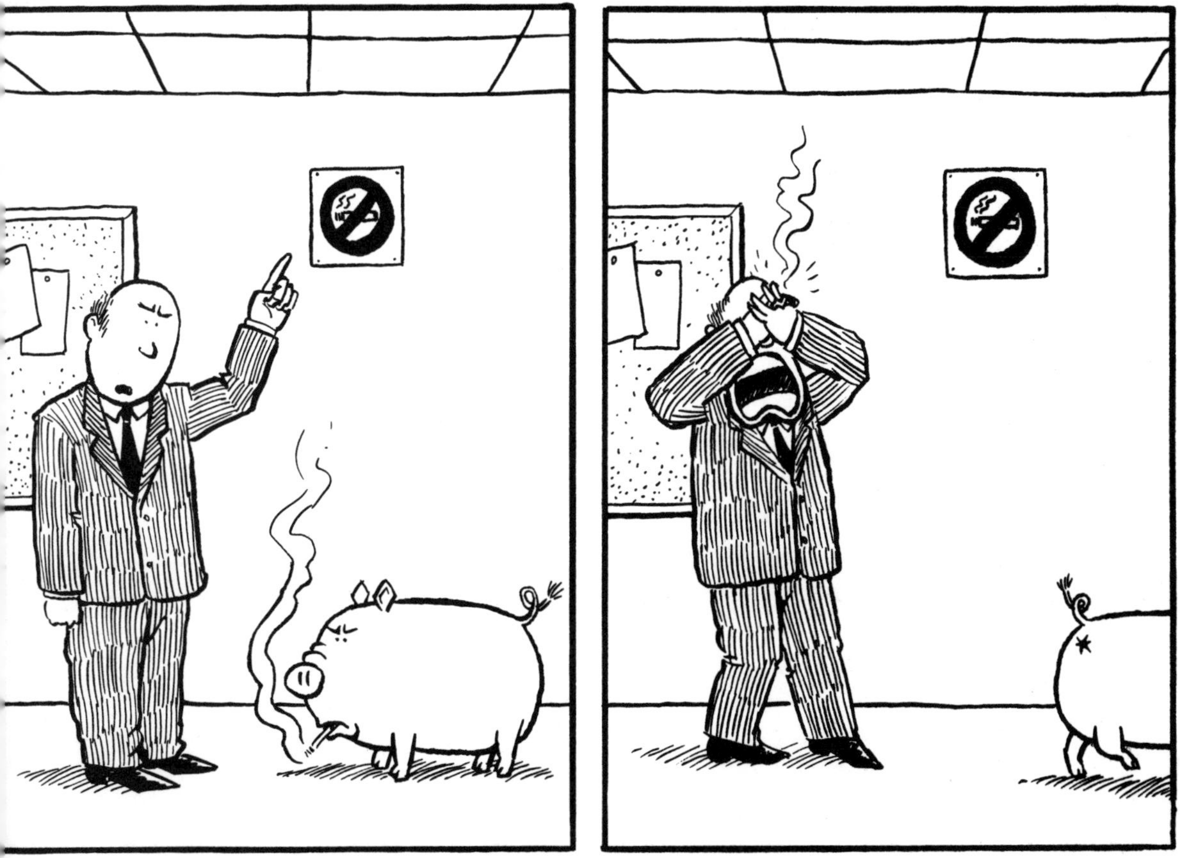

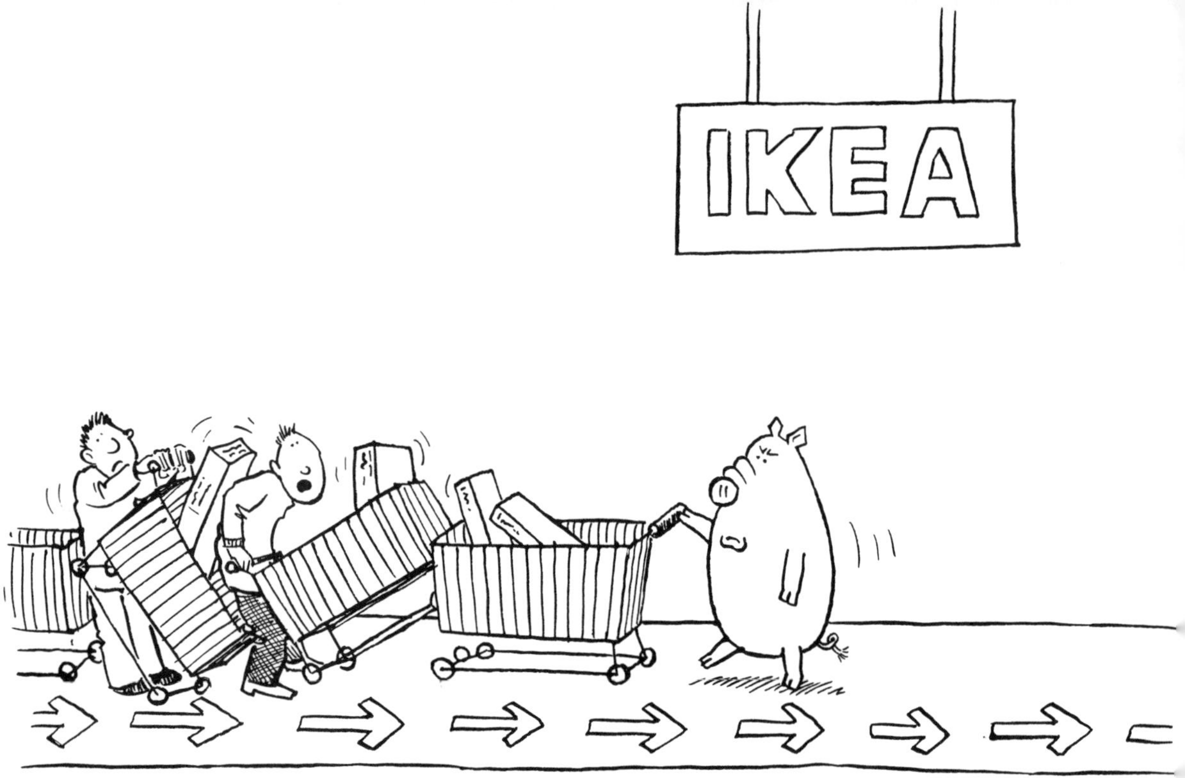
IKEA

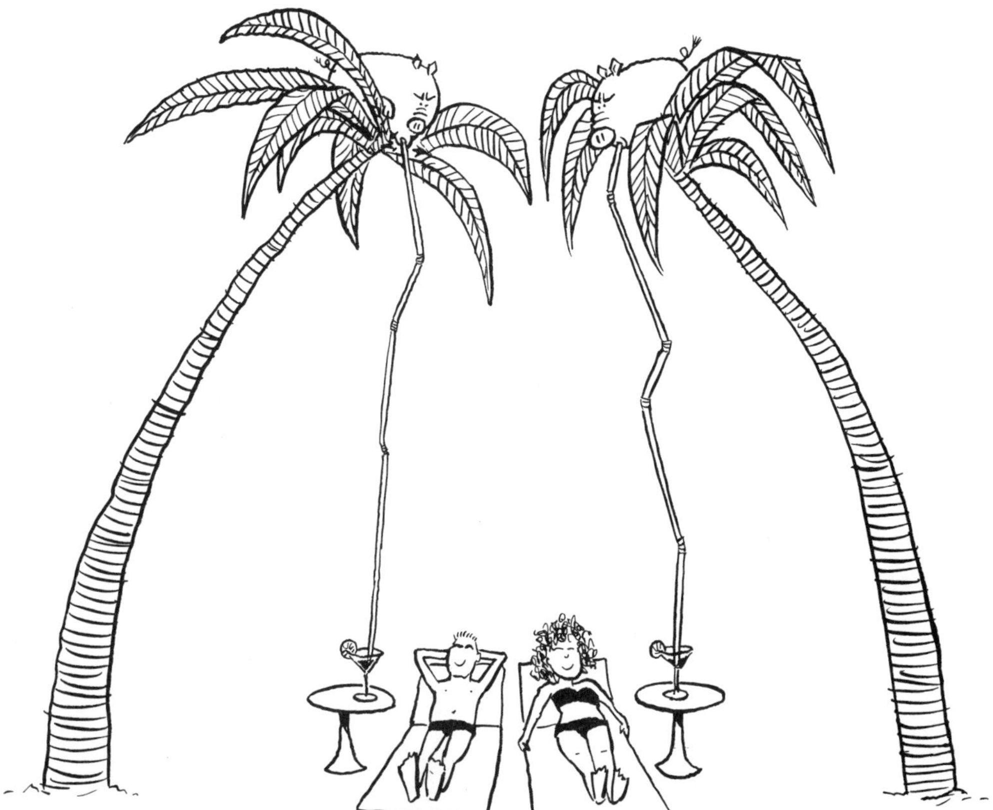

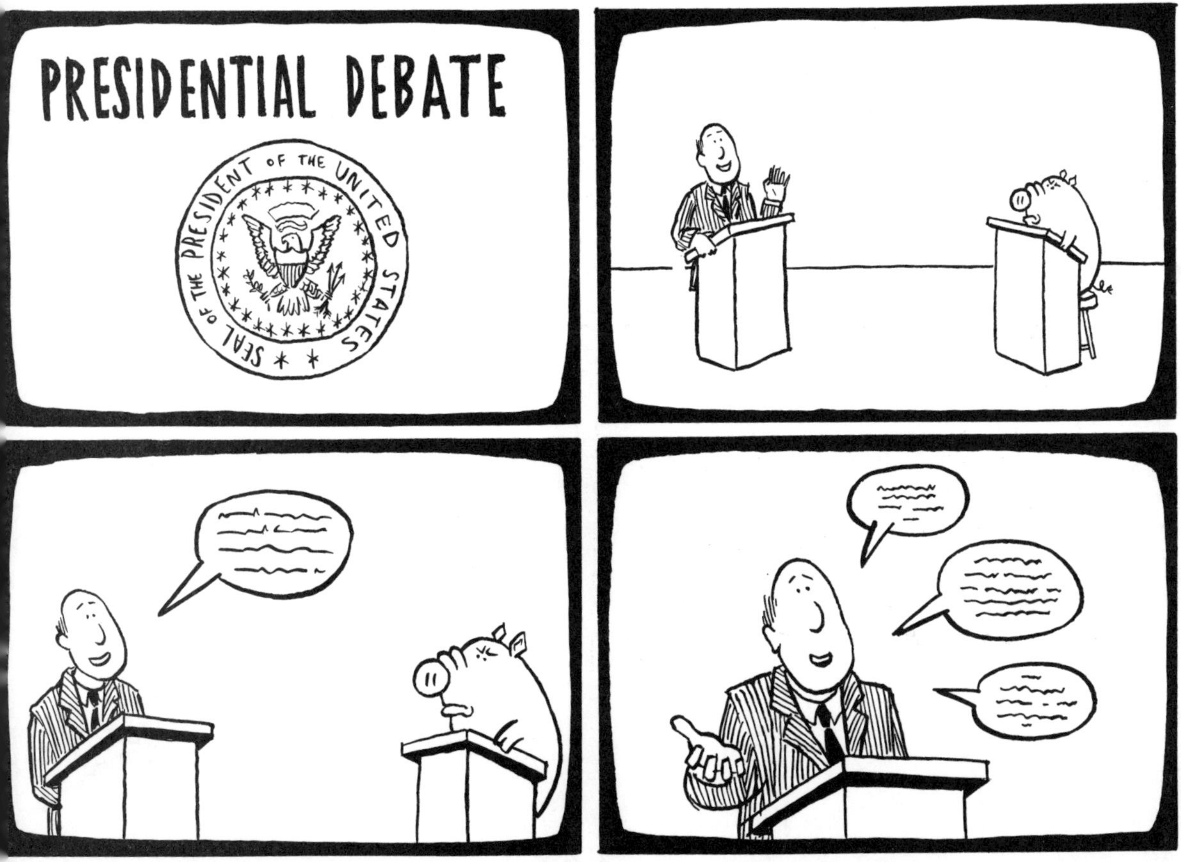
PRESIDENTIAL DEBATE
SEAL OF THE PRESIDENT OF THE UNITED STATES

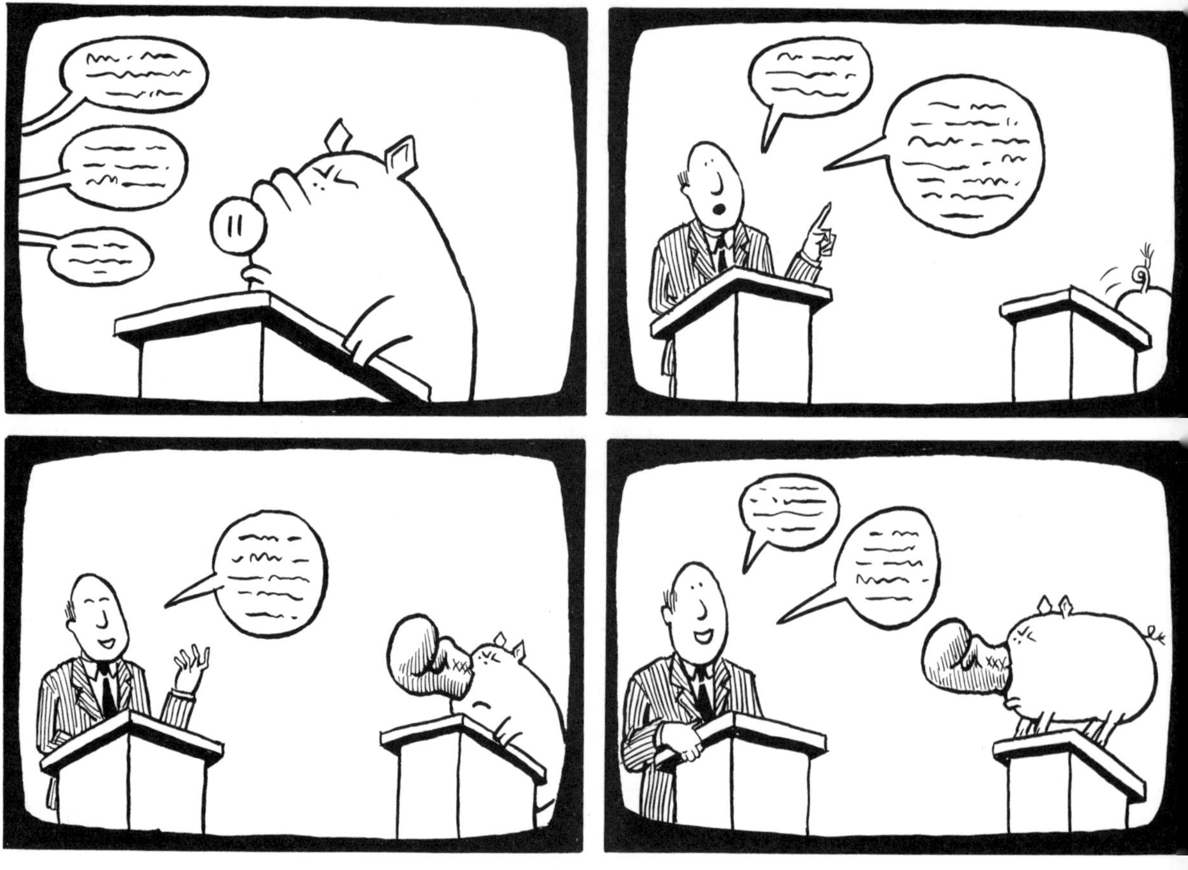

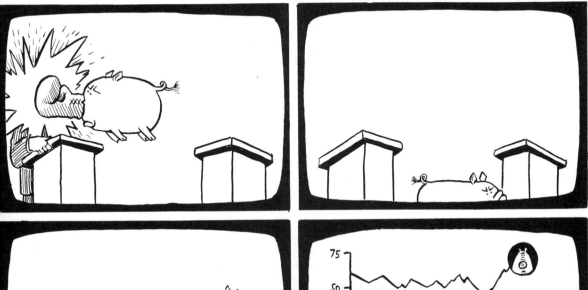

% APPROVAL RATING

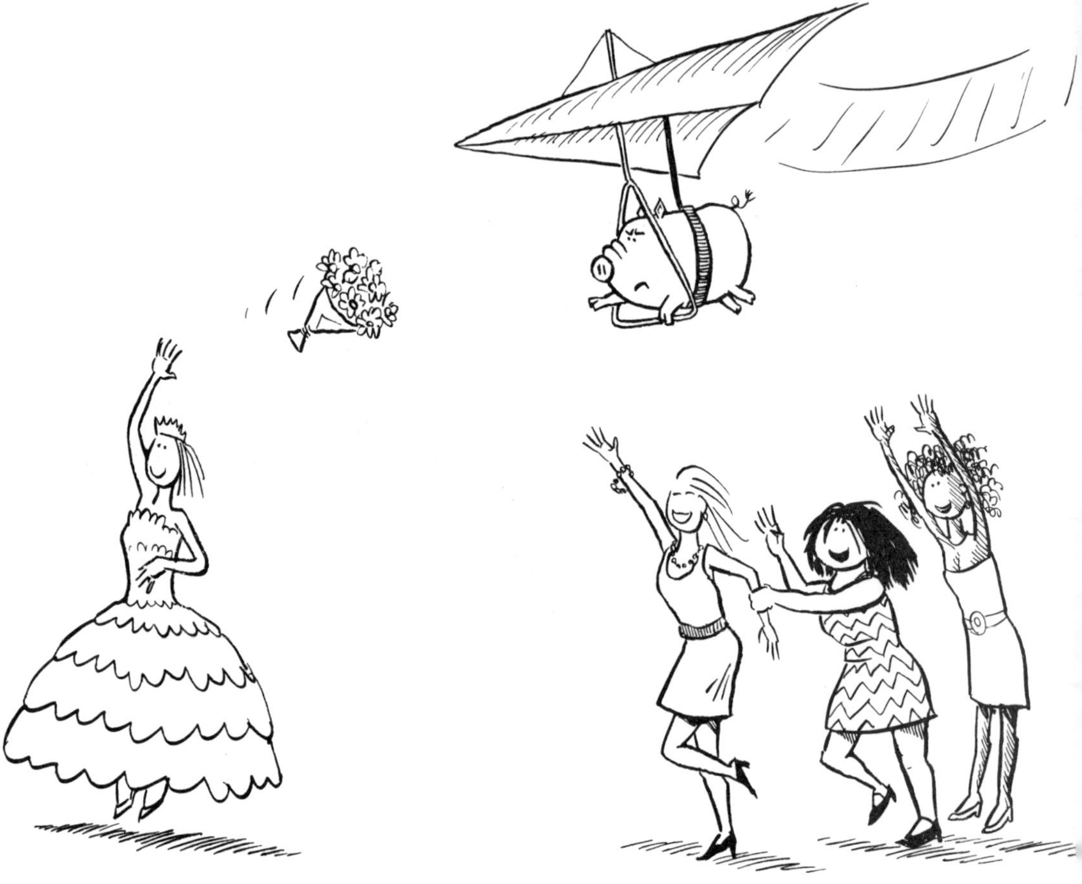

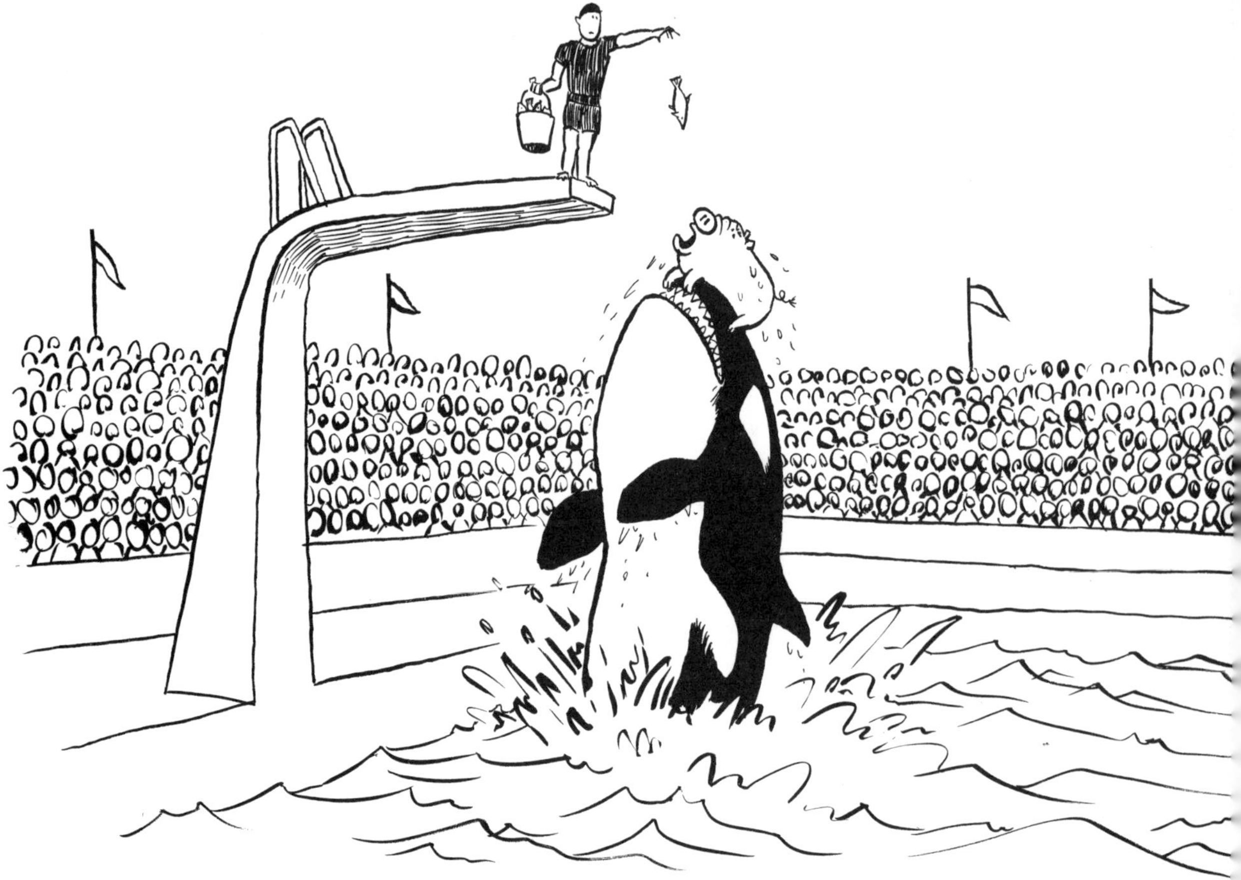

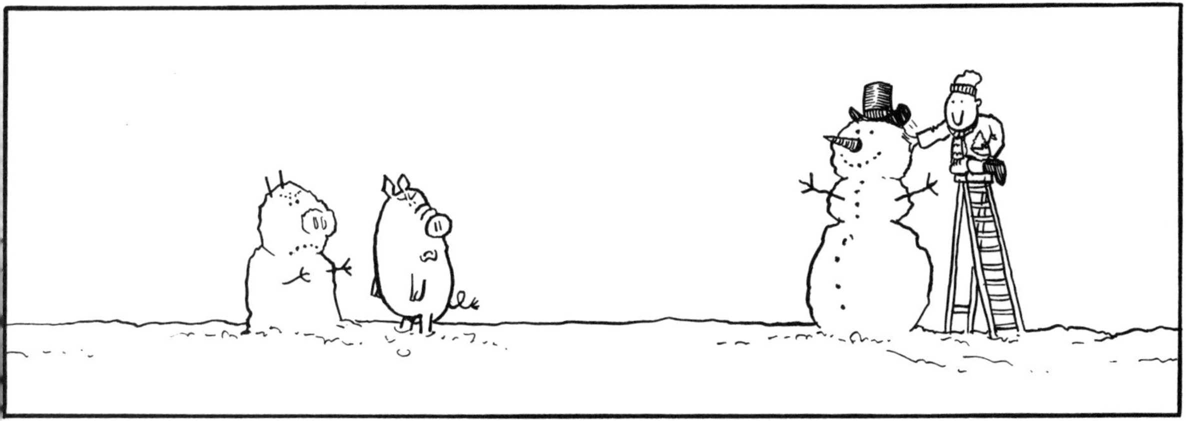

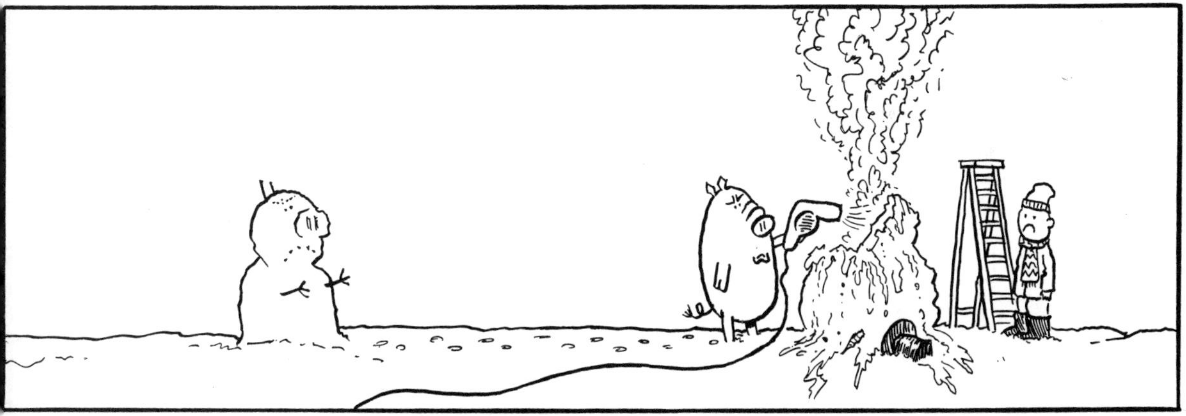

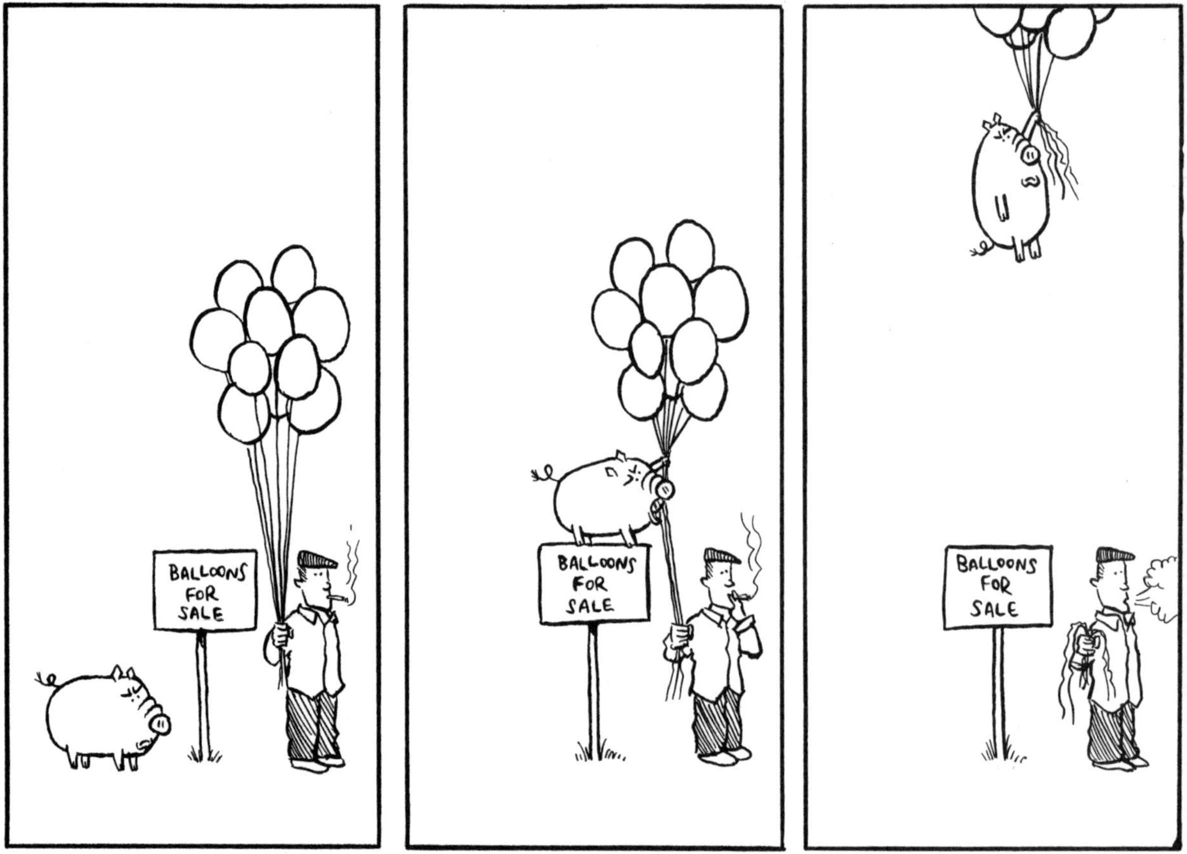
BALLOONS FOR SALE
BALLOONS FOR SALE
BALLOONS FOR SALE

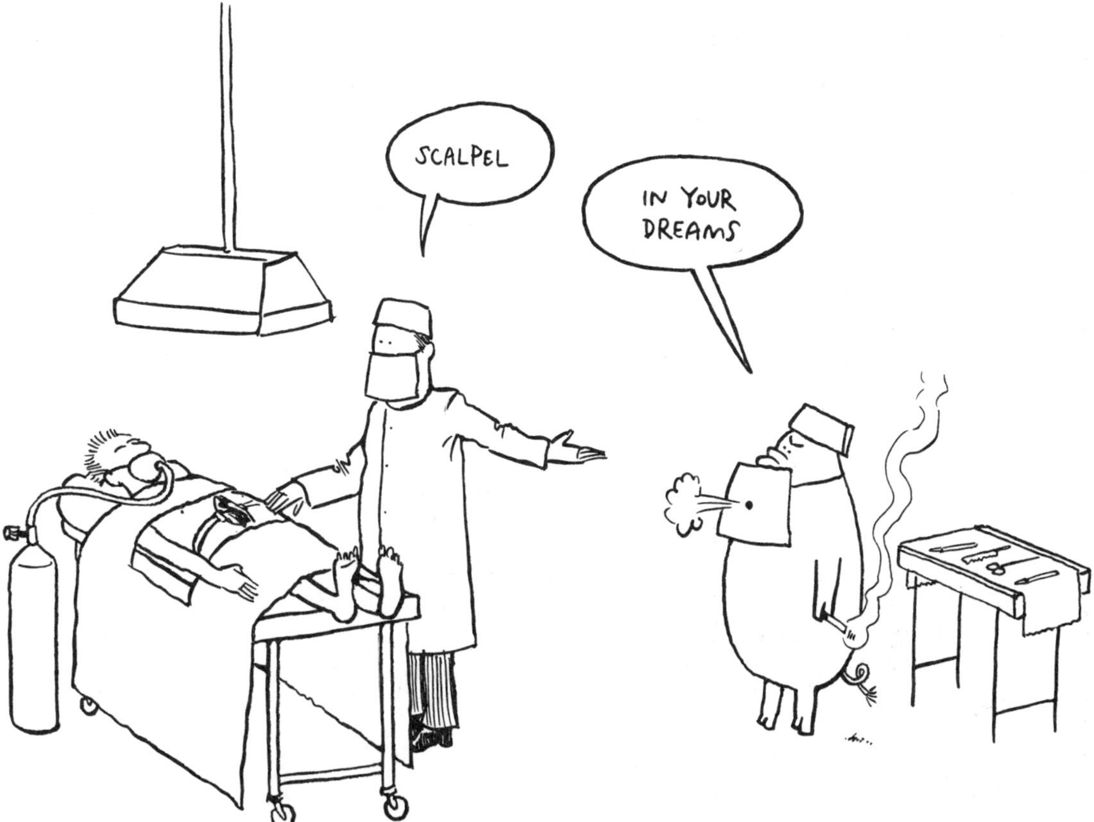
SCALPEL
IN YOUR DREAMS

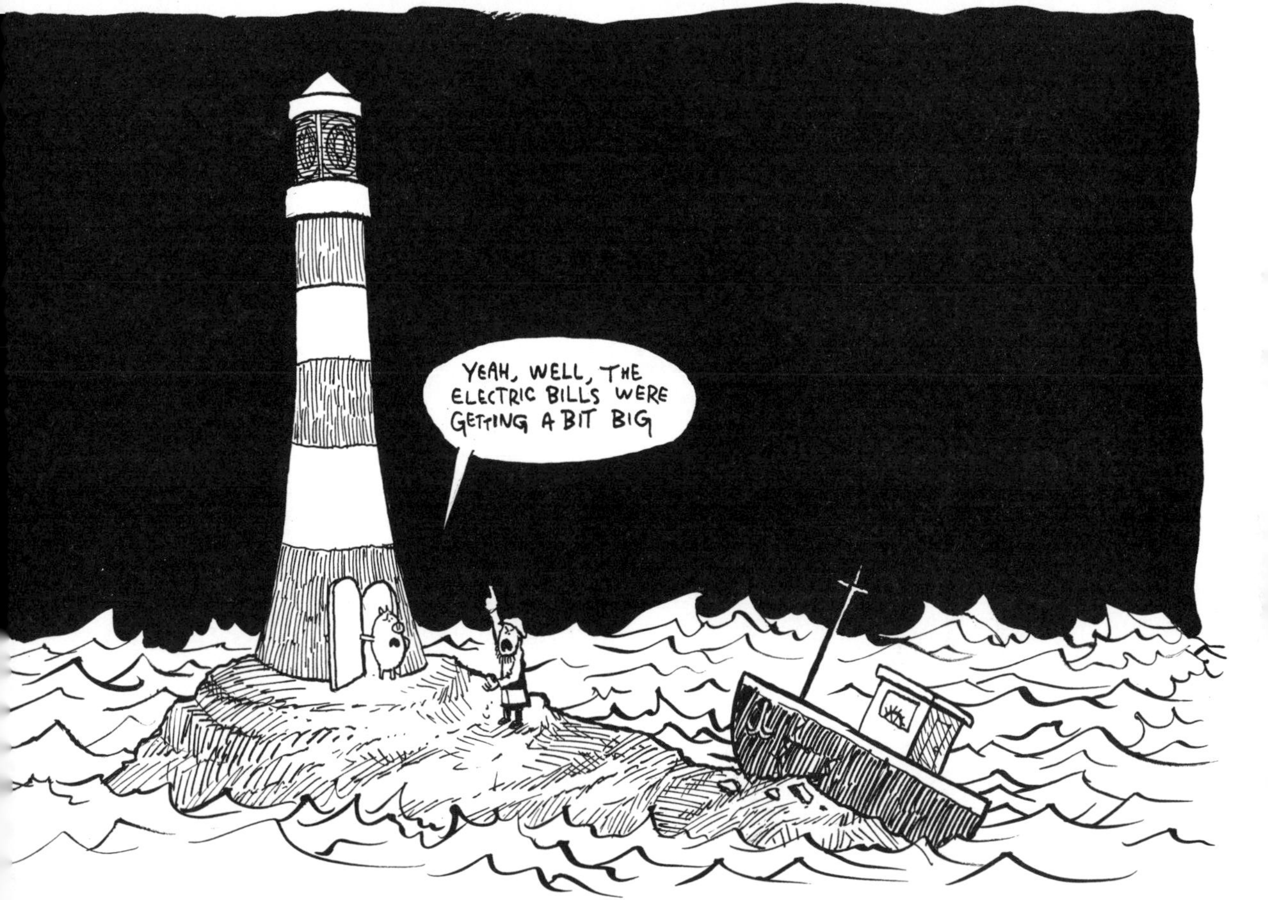
YEAH, WELL, THE ELECTRIC BILLS WERE GETTING A BIT BIG

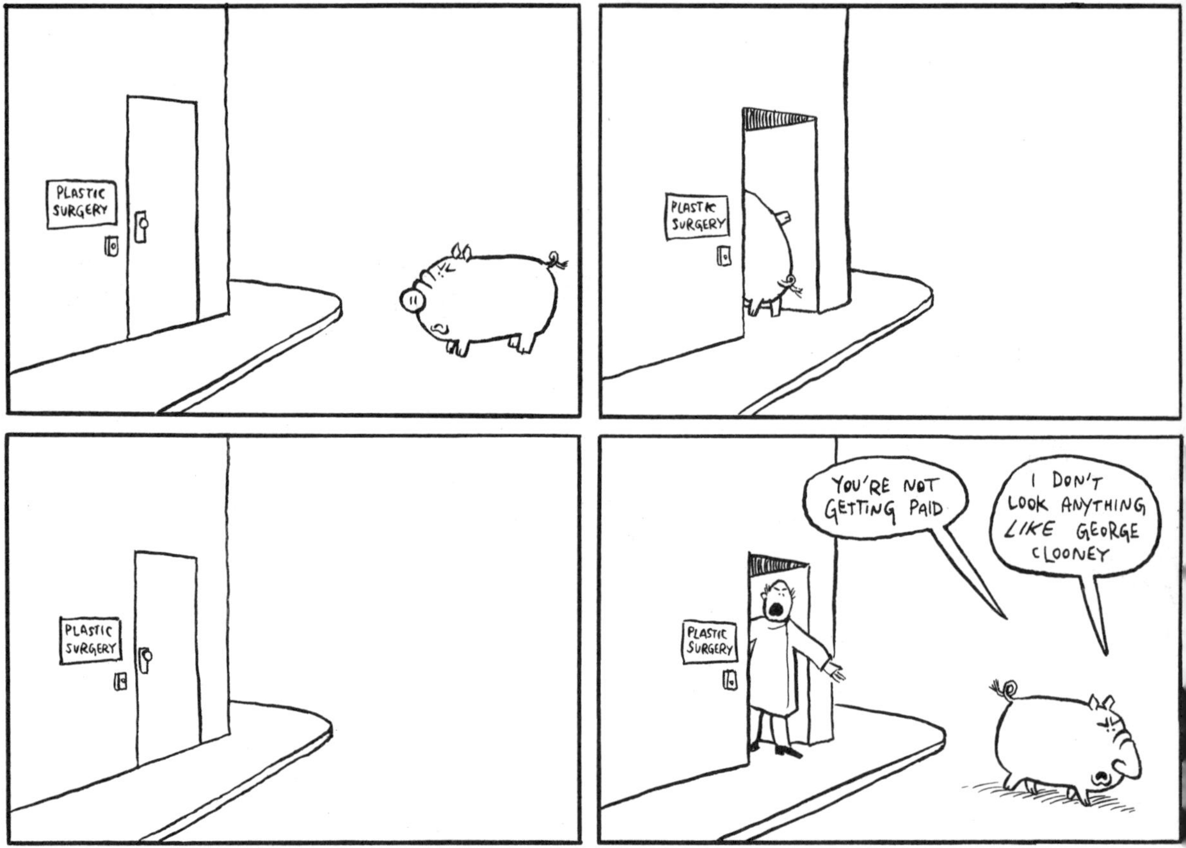
PLASTIC SURGERY
PLASTIC SURGERY
PLASTIC SURGERY
PLASTIC SURGERY
YOU'RE NOT GETTING PAID
I DON'T LOOK ANYTHING LIKE GEORGE CLOONEY

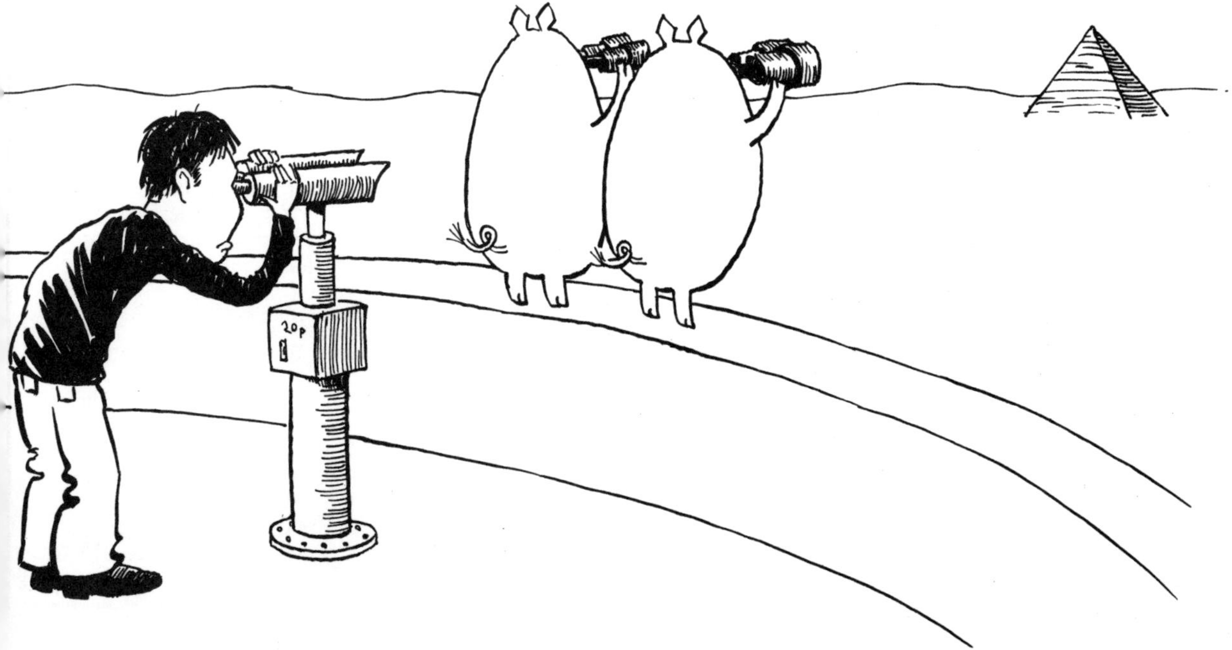
20p

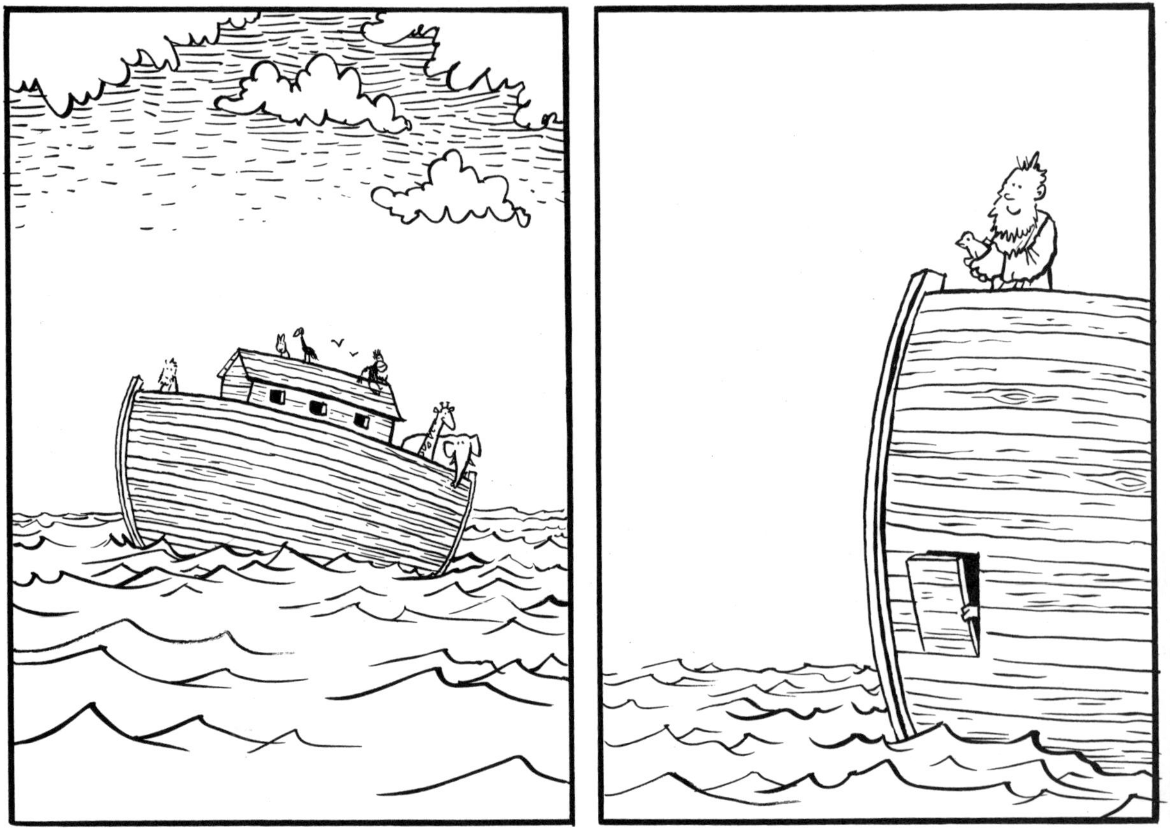

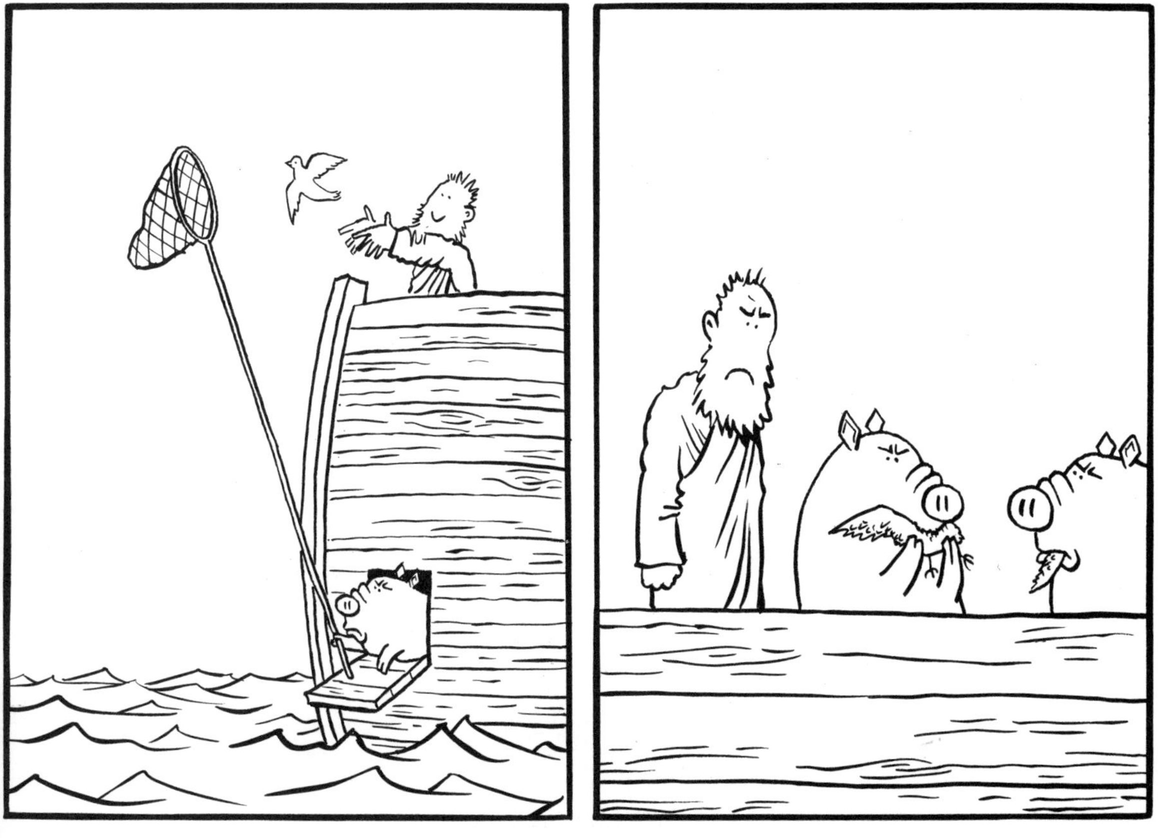

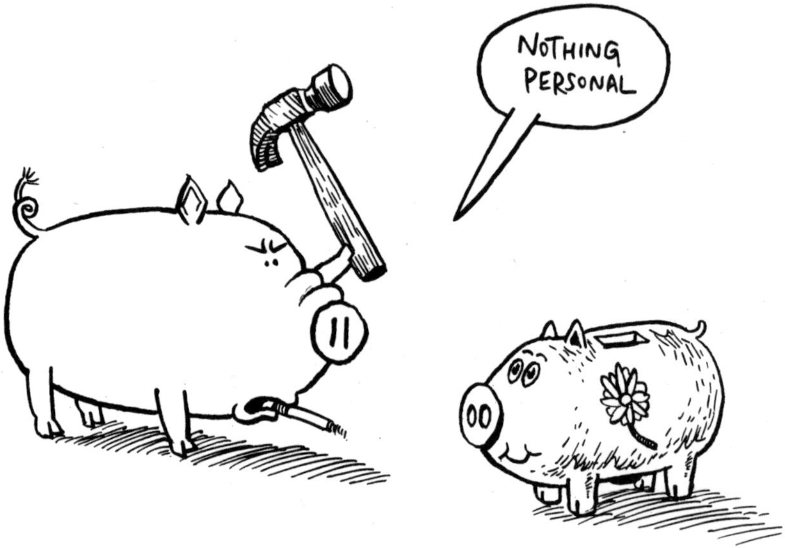
NOTHING PERSONAL

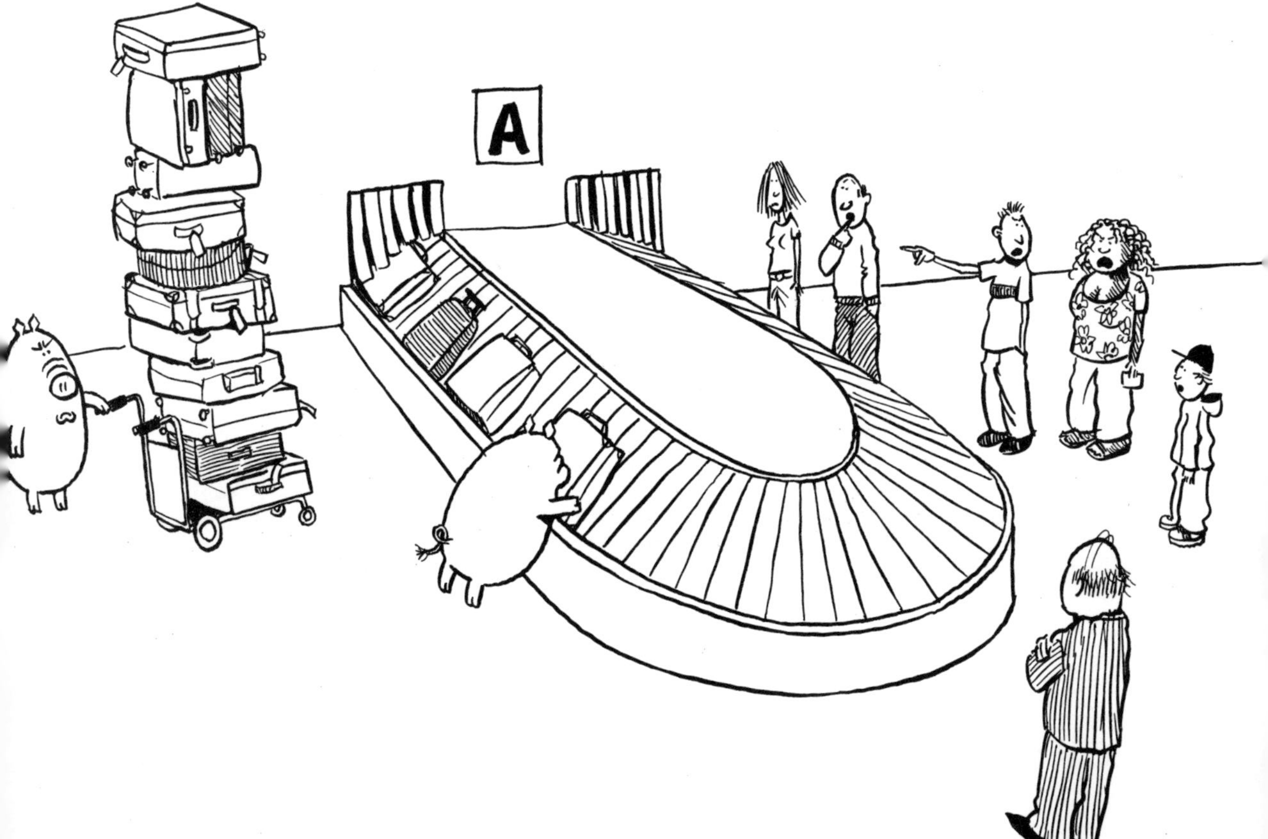
A

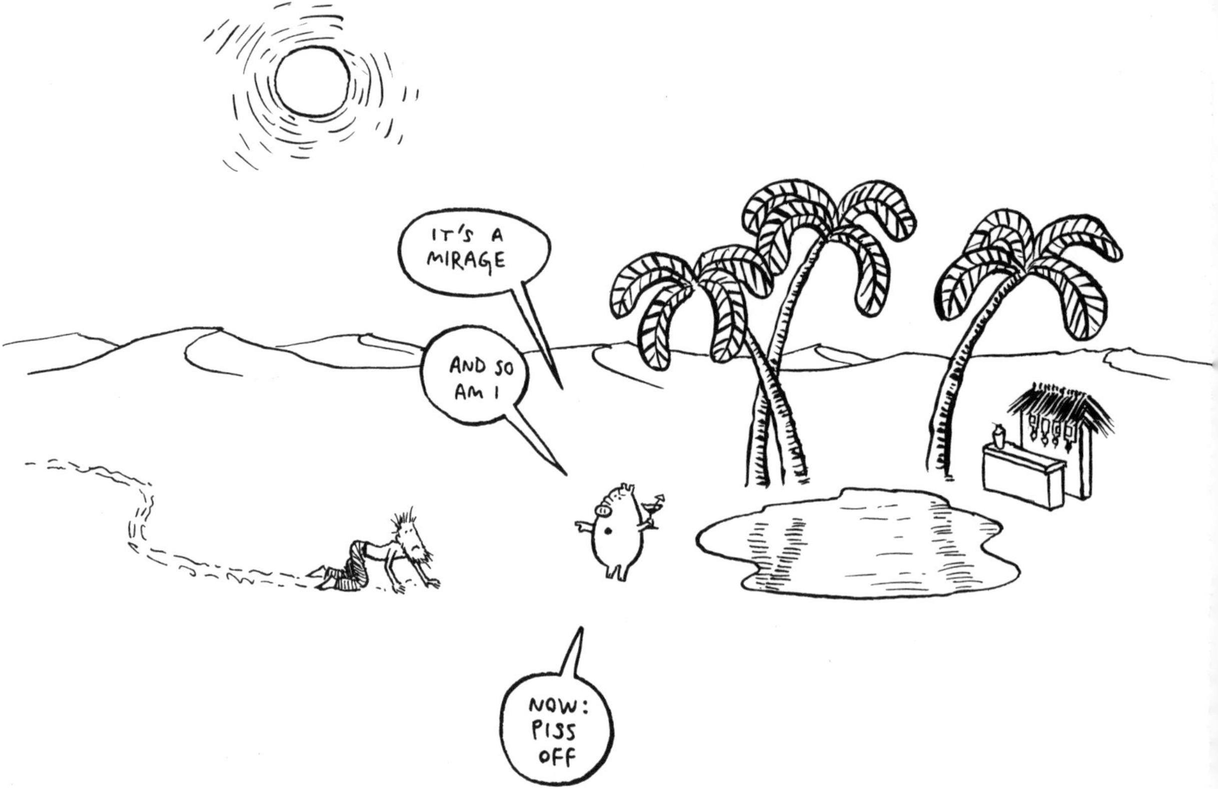
IT'S A MIRAGE
AND SO AM I
NOW: PISS OFF

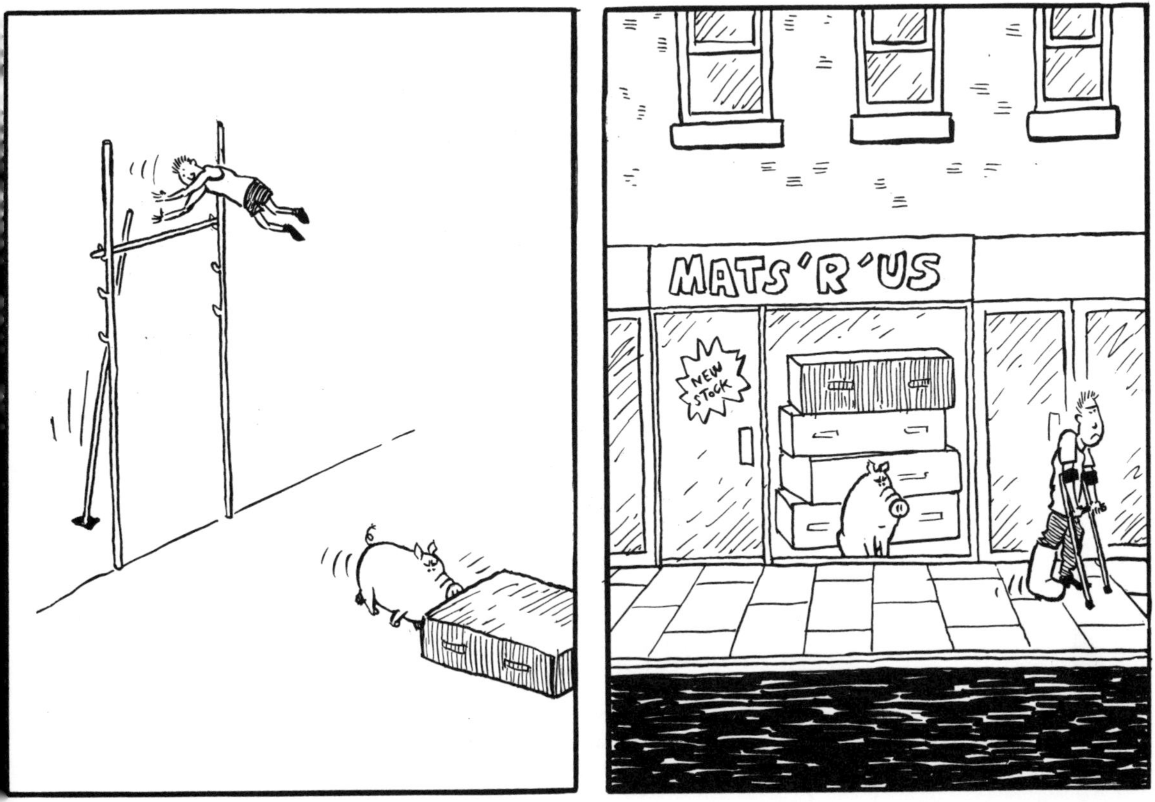
MATS 'R' US
NEW STOCK

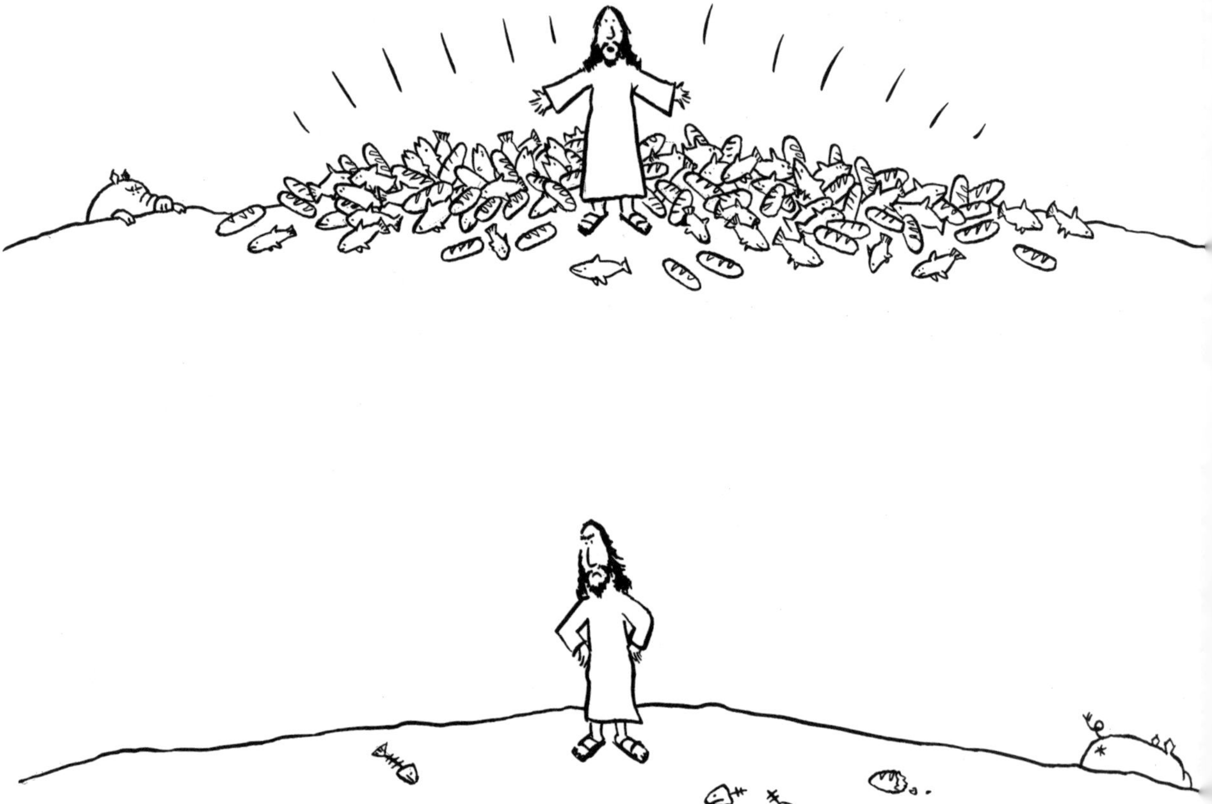

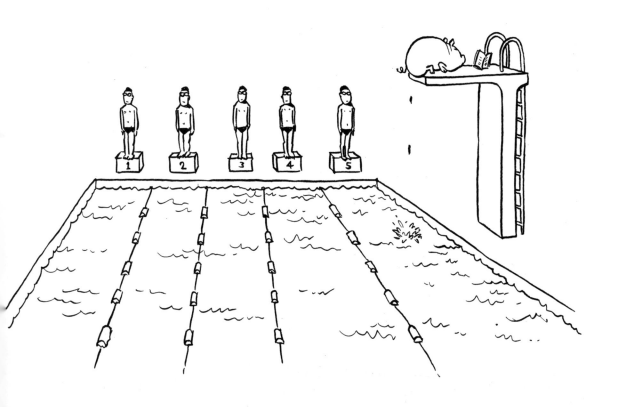

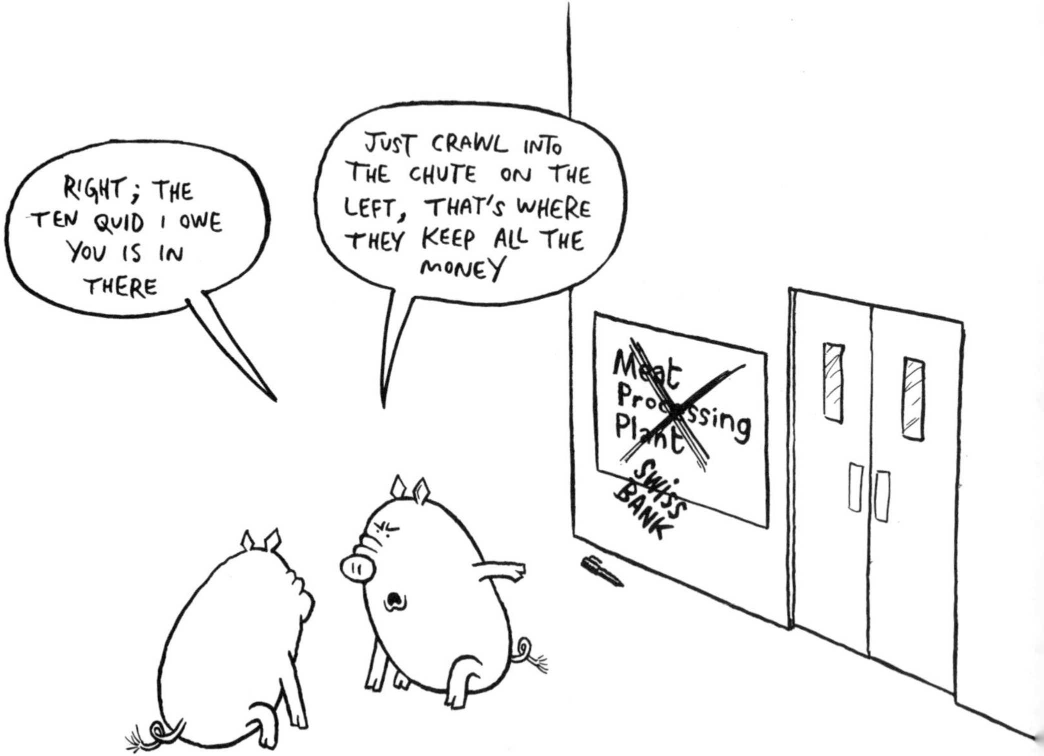
RIGHT; THE TEN QUID I OWE YOU IS IN THERE
JUST CRAWL INTO THE CHUTE ON THE LEFT, THAT'S WHERE THEY KEEP ALL THE MONEY
Meat Processing Plant
SWISS BANK

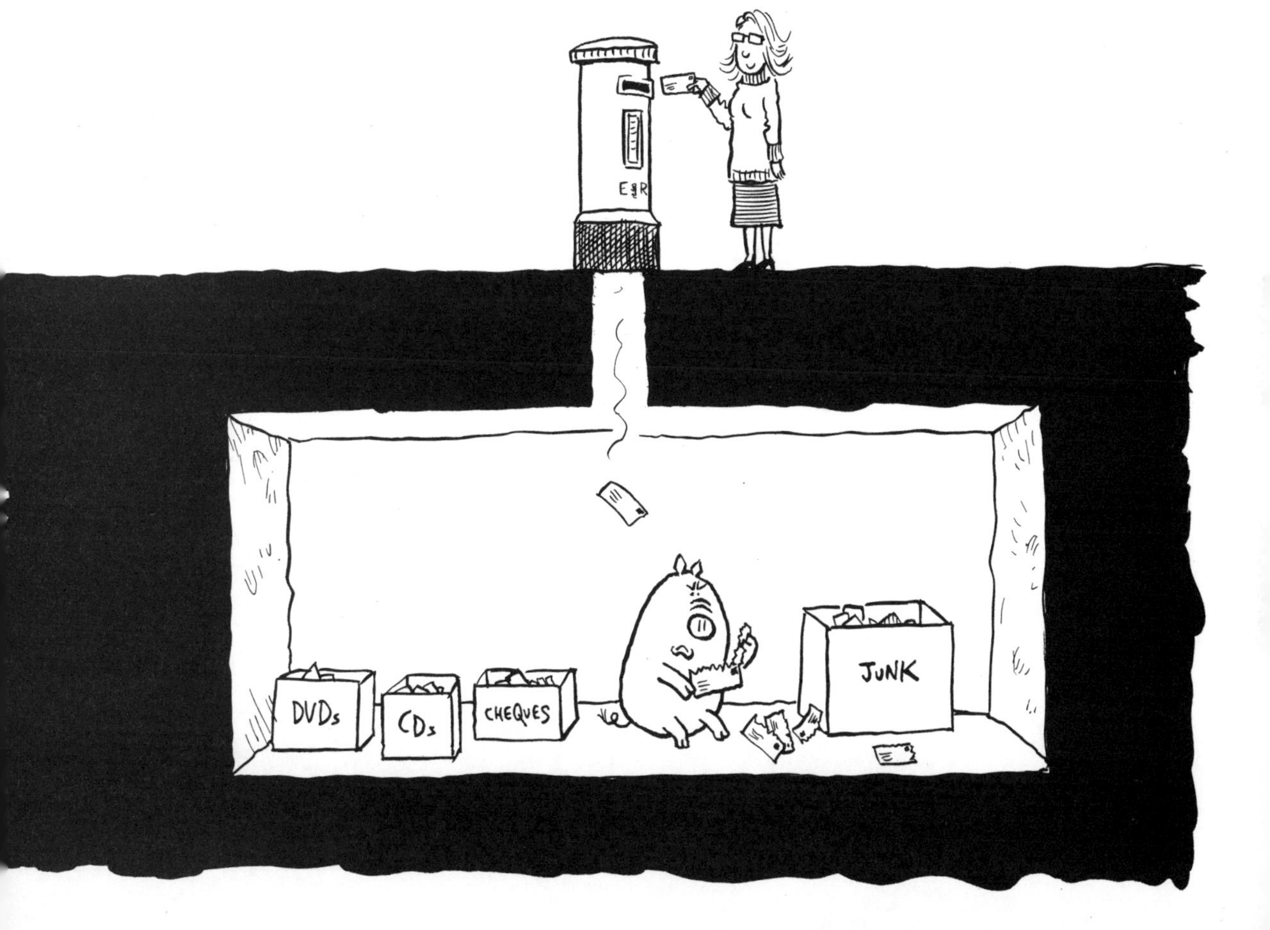
DVDs
CDs
CHEQUES
JUNK

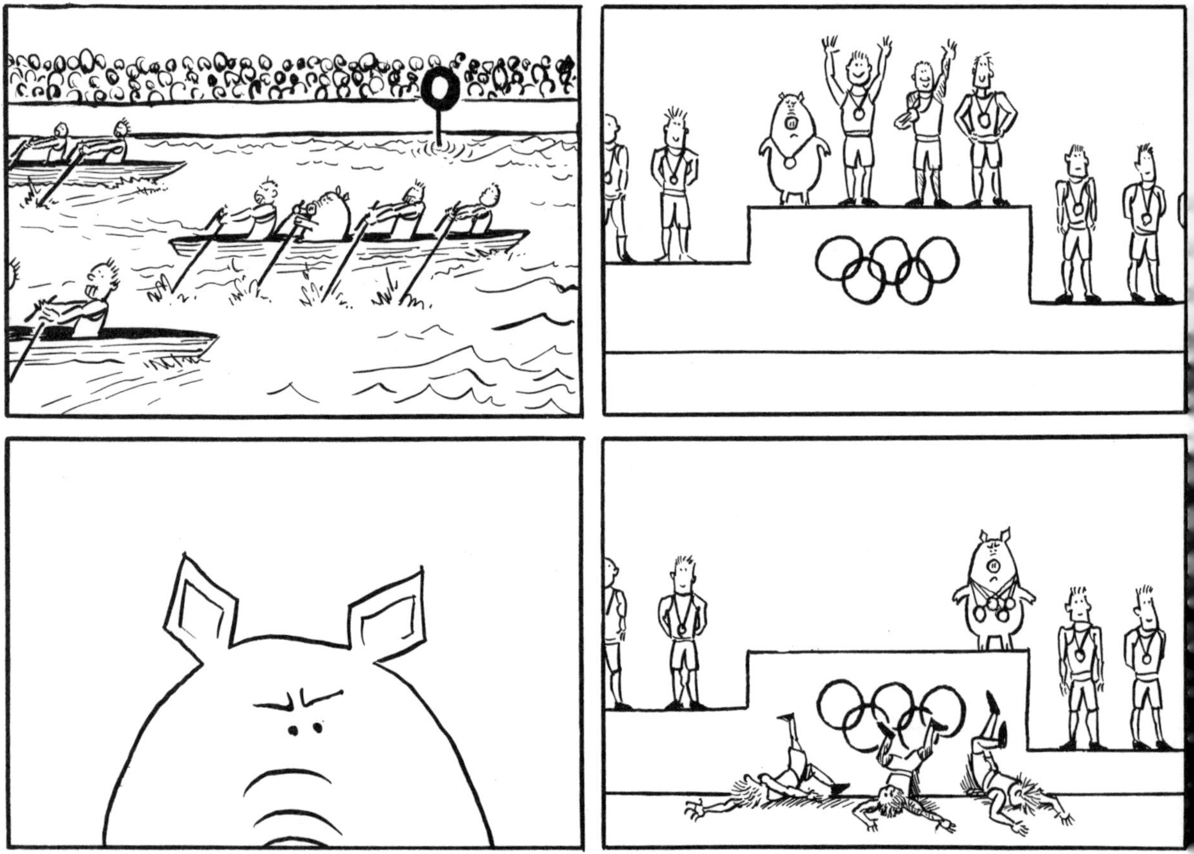

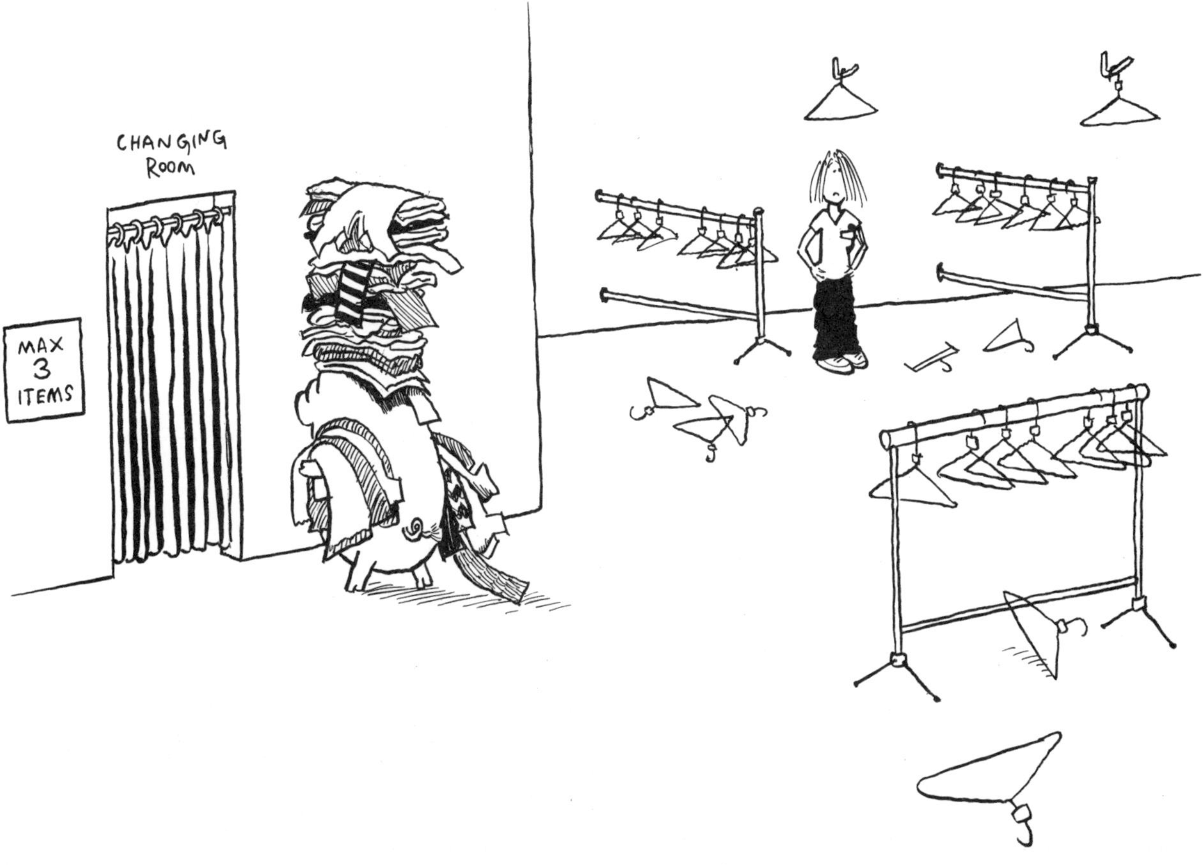
CHANGING ROOM
MAX 3 ITEMS

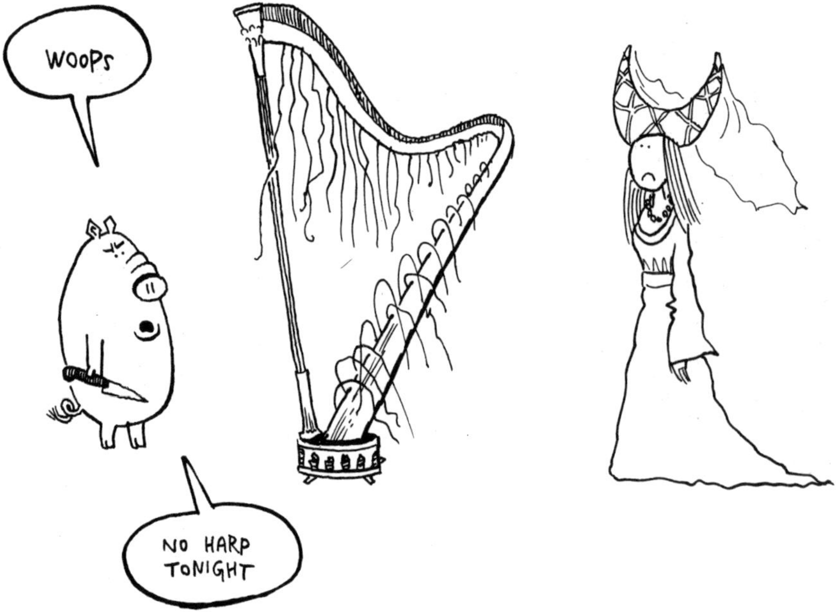
WOOPS
NO HARP TONIGHT

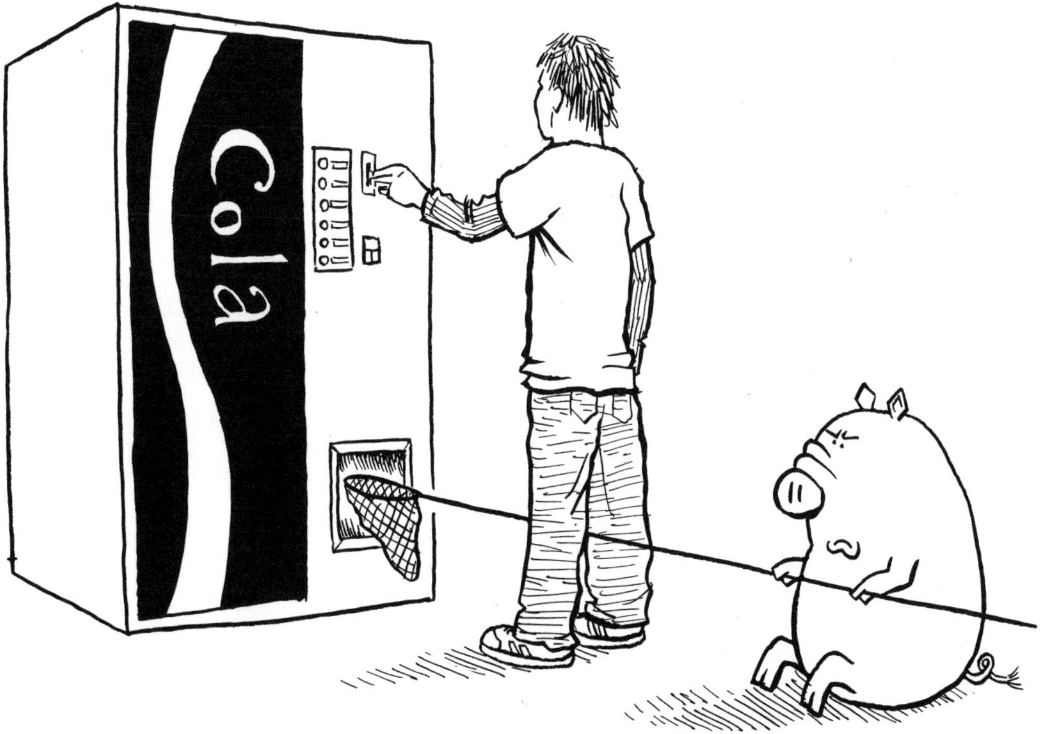
Cola

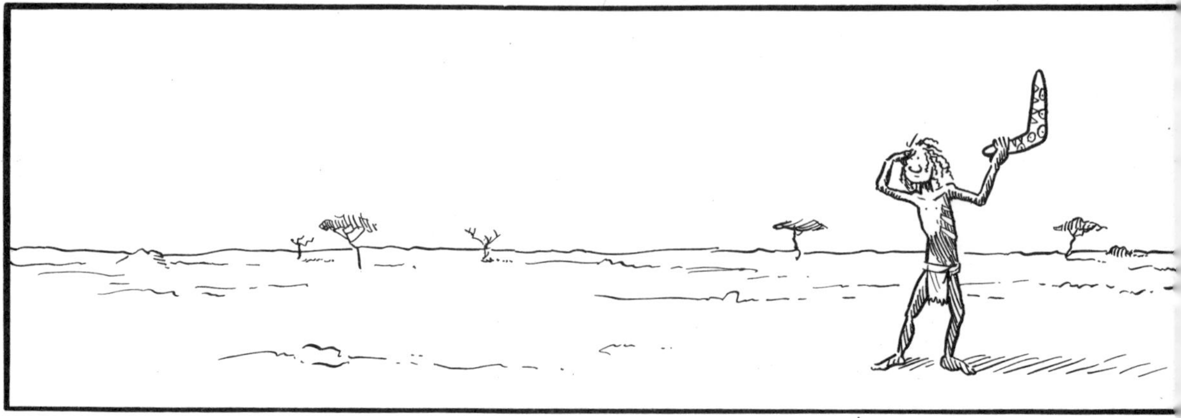

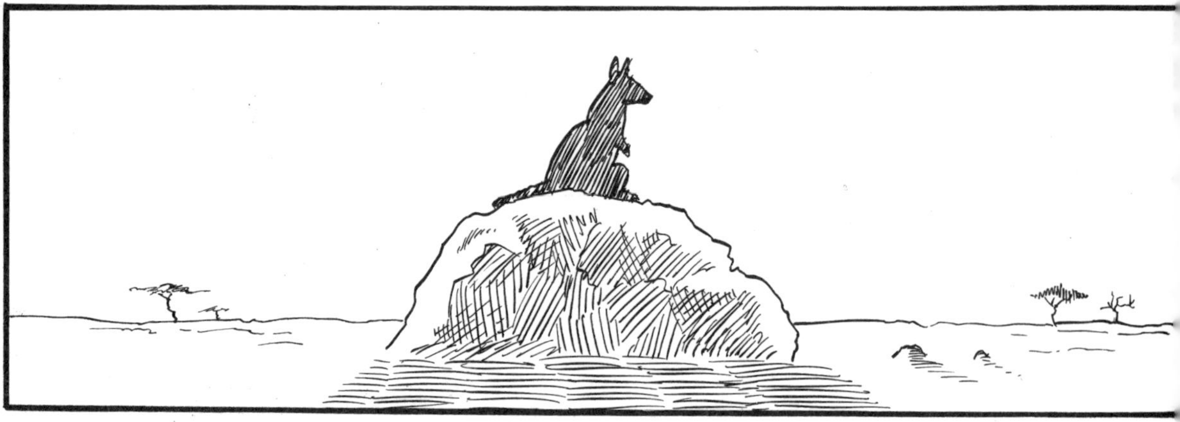

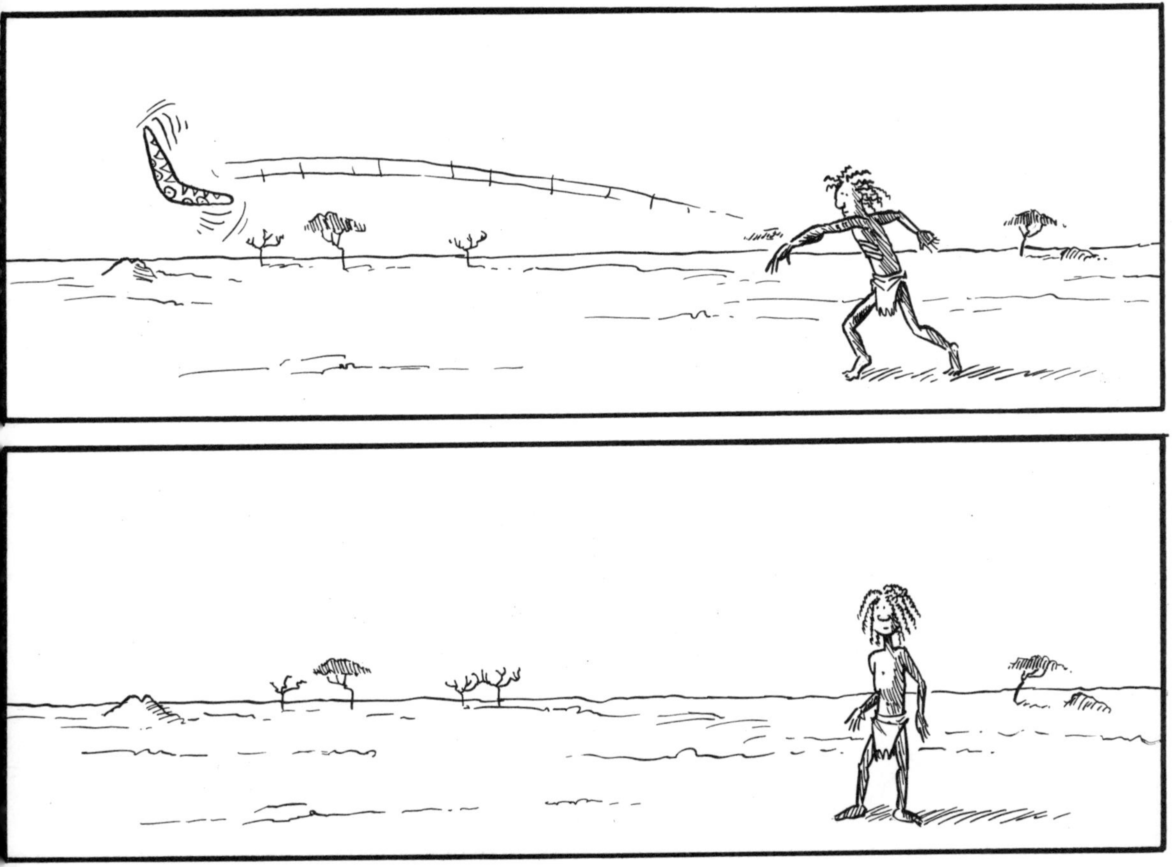

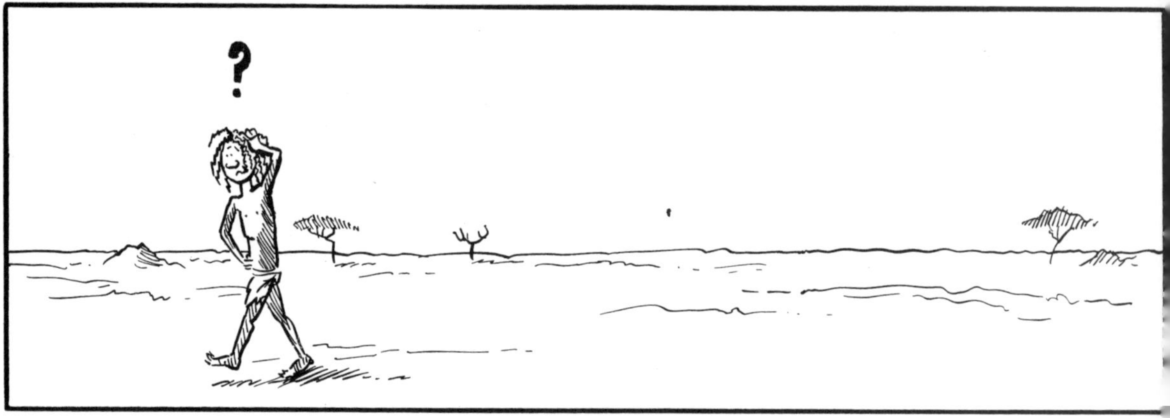
?

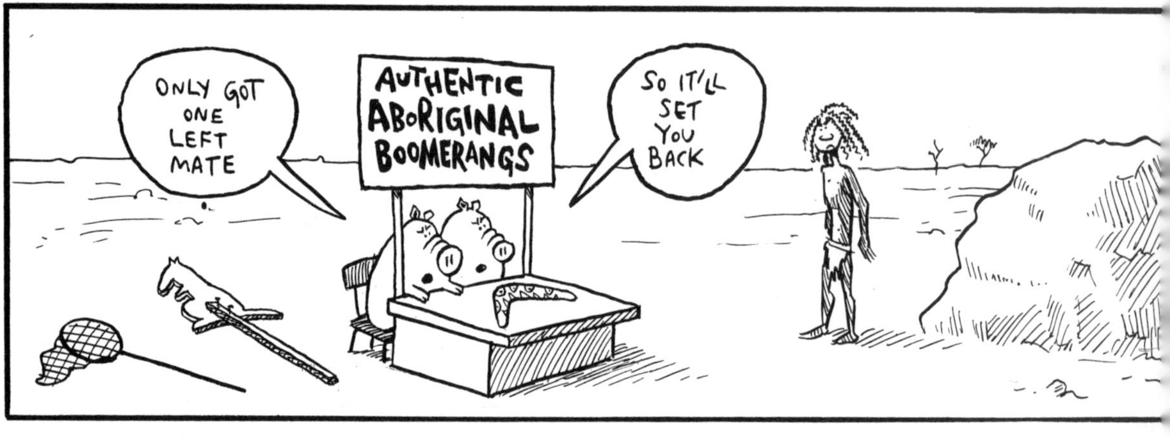
ONLY GOT ONE LEFT MATE
AUTHENTIC ABORIGINAL BOOMERANGS
SO IT'LL SET YOU BACK

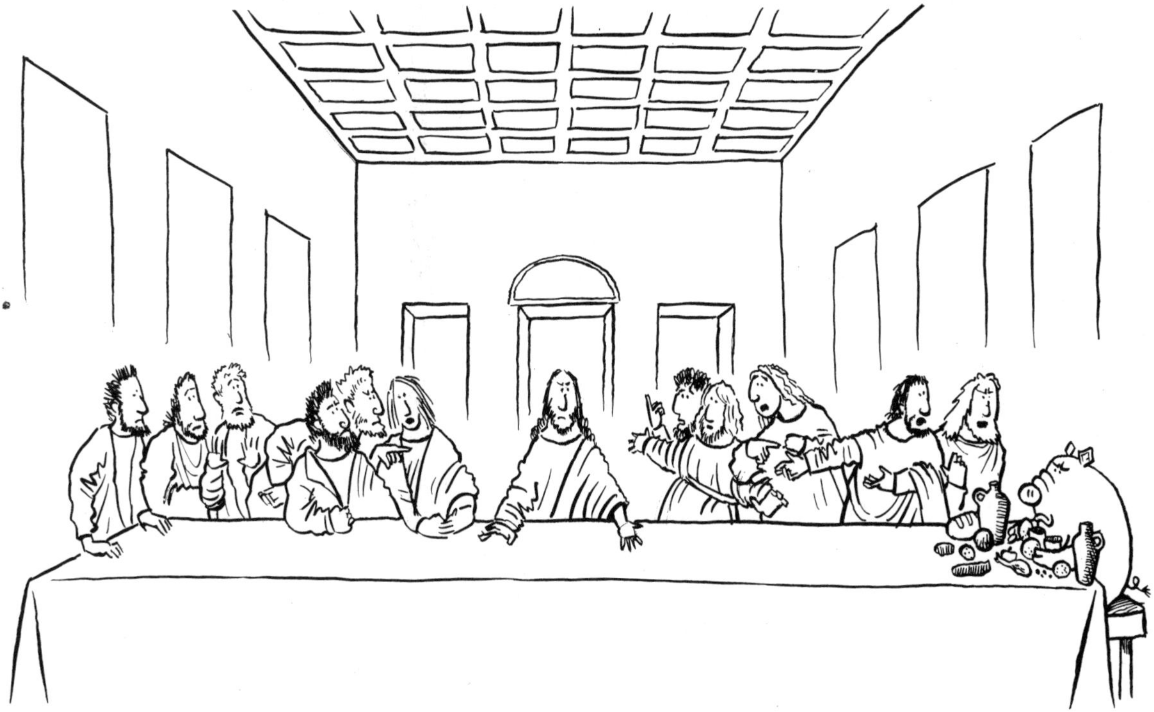

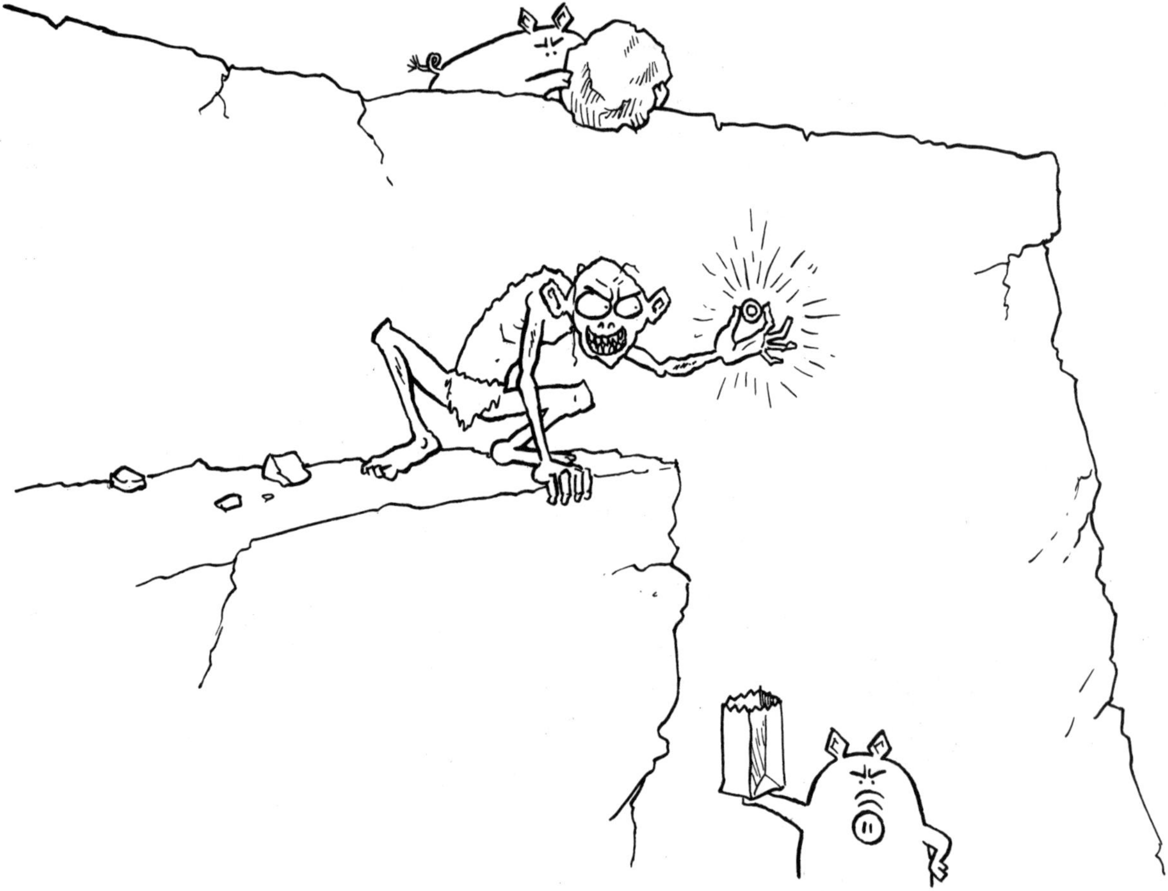

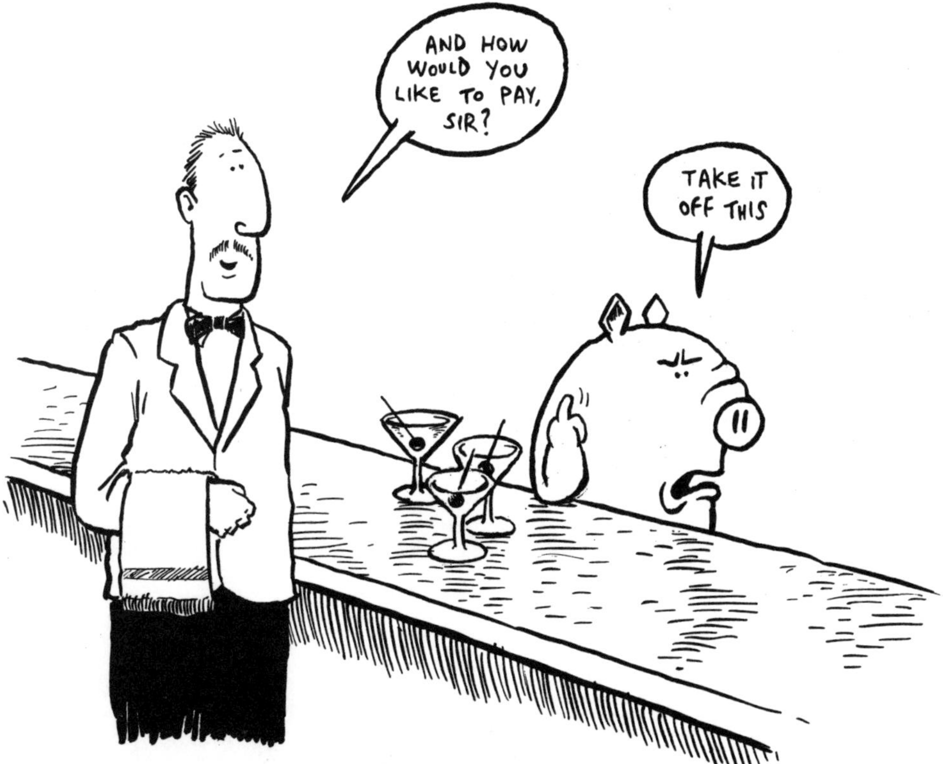
AND HOW WOULD YOU LIKE TO PAY, SIR?
TAKE IT OFF THIS

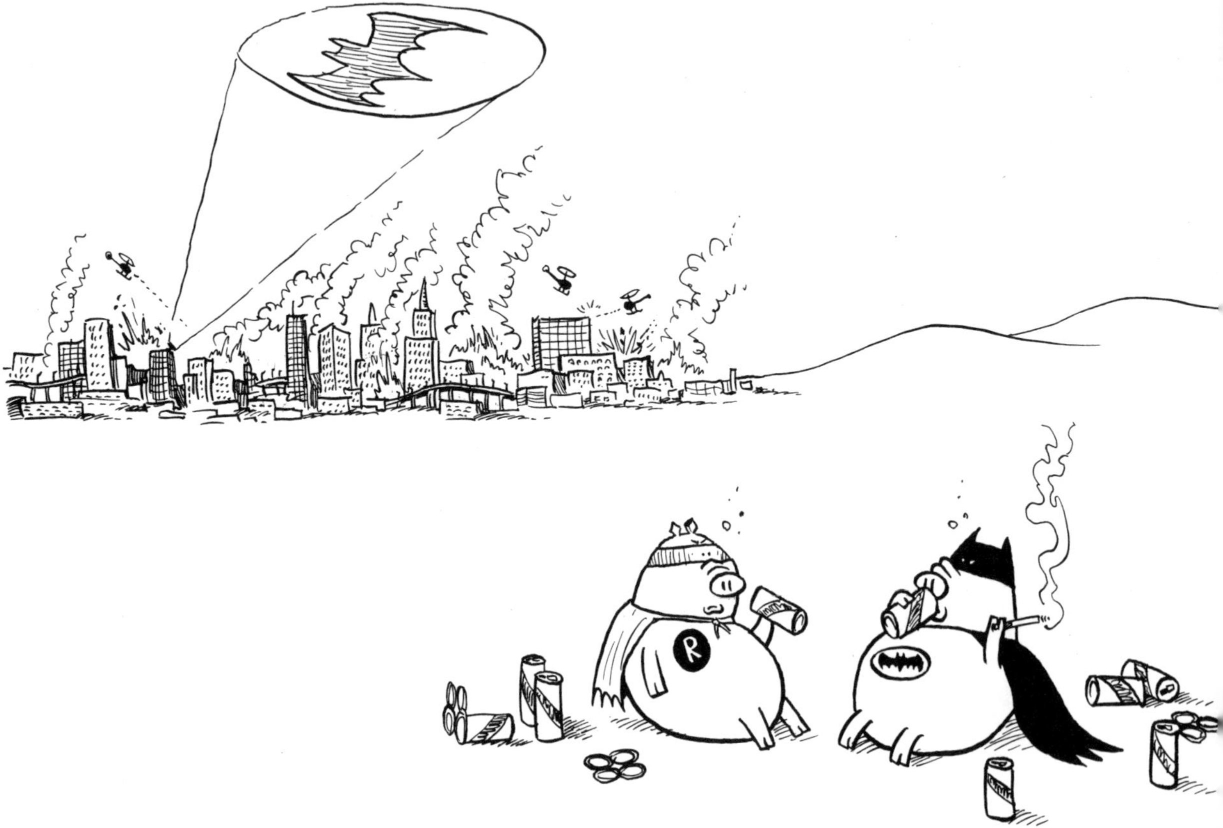

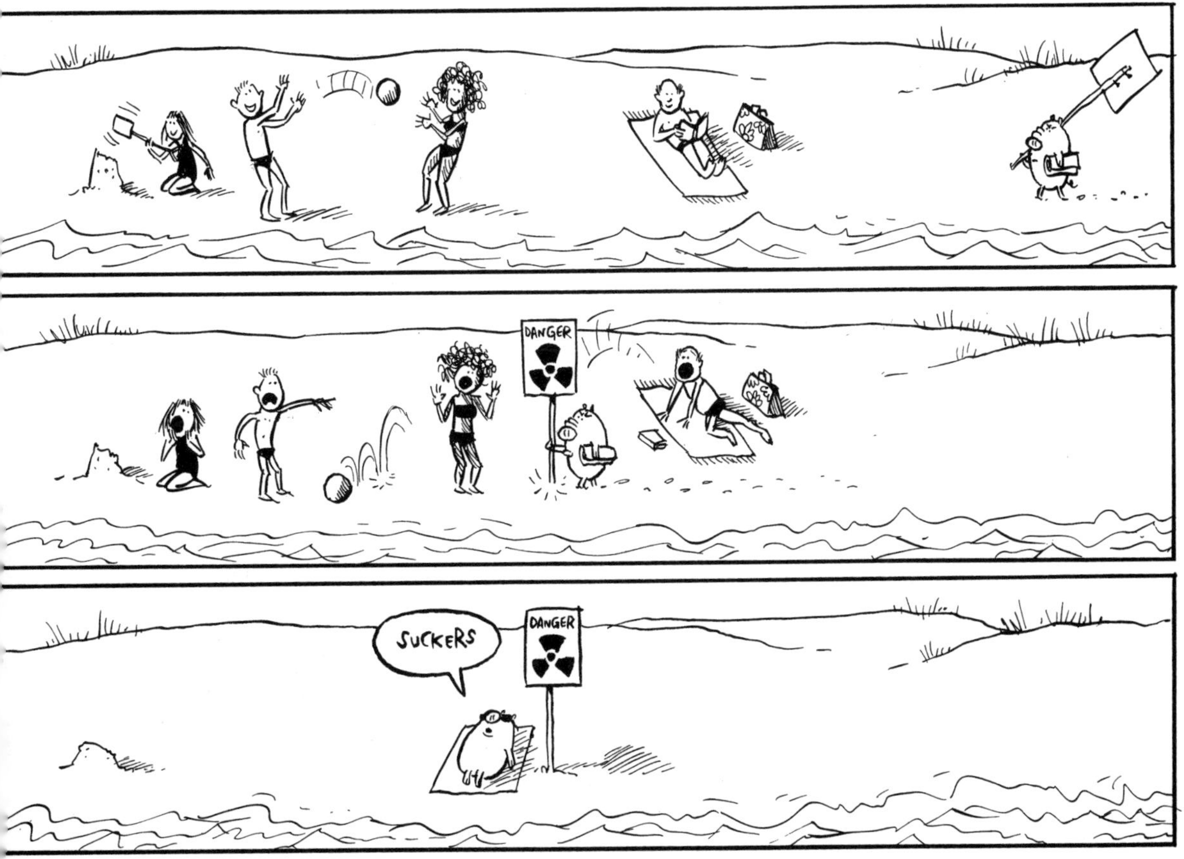
DANGER
DANGER
SUCKERS

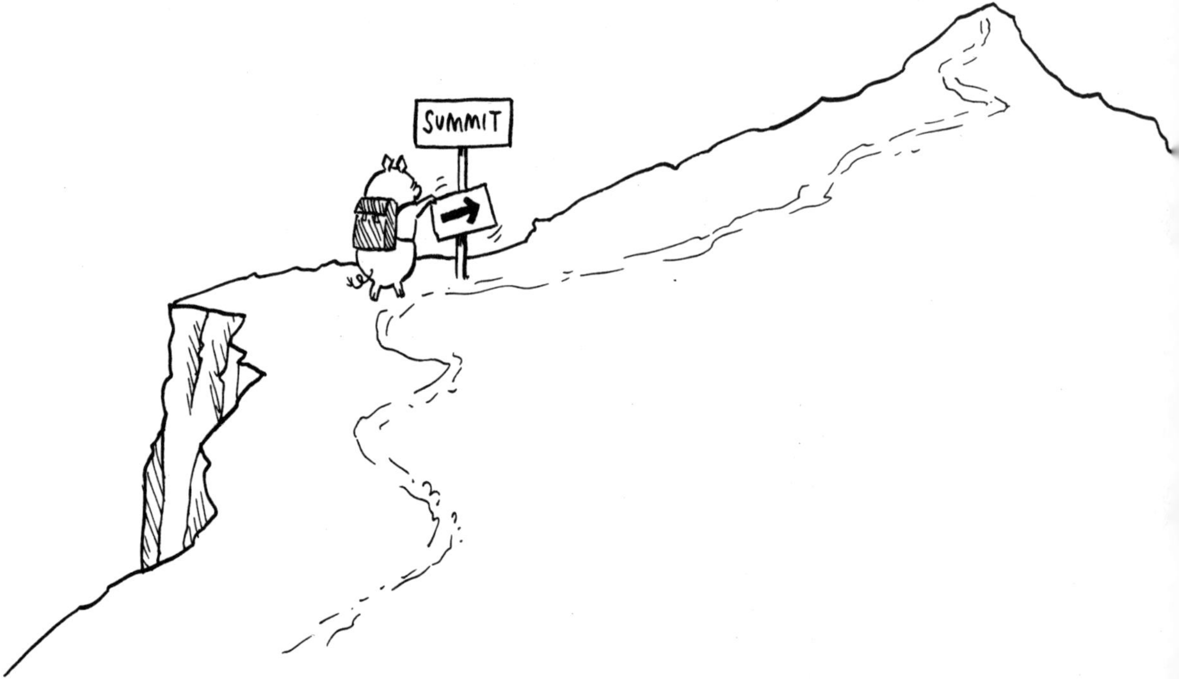
SUMMIT

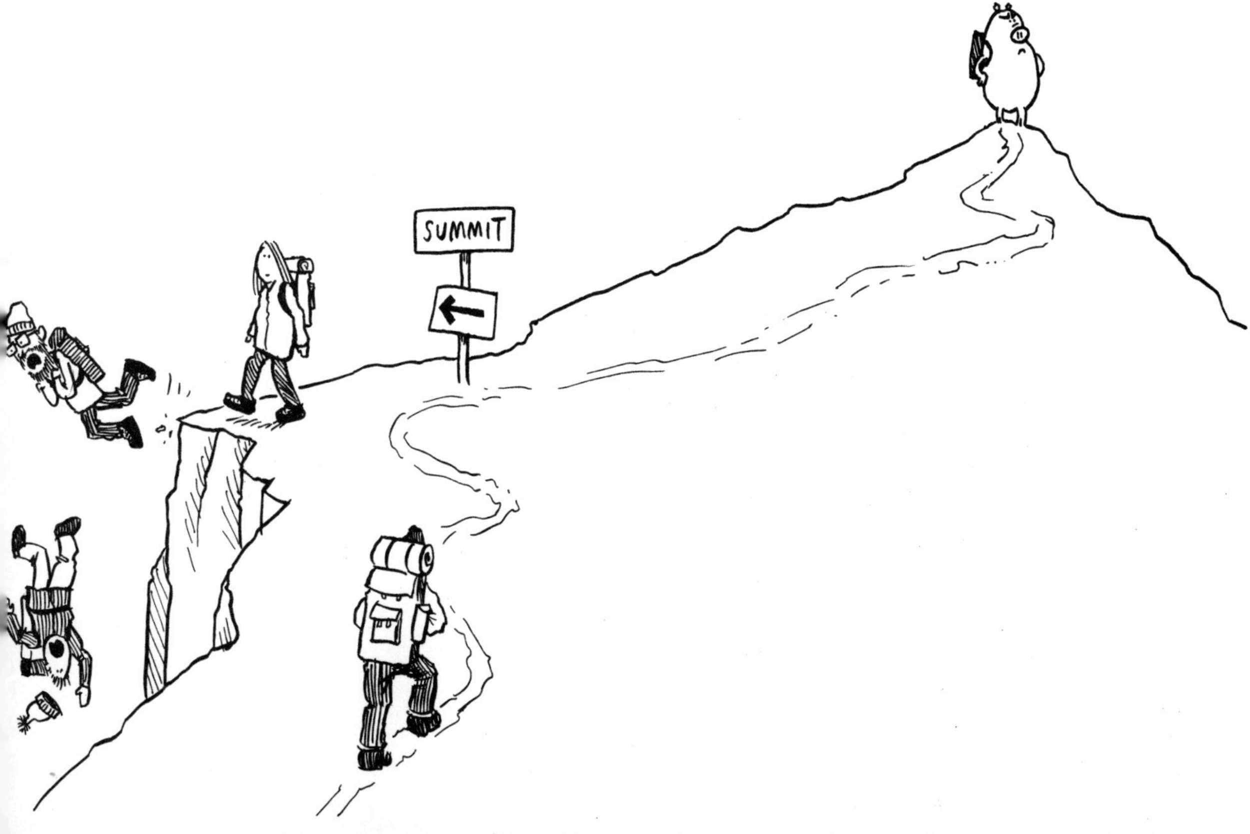
SUMMIT

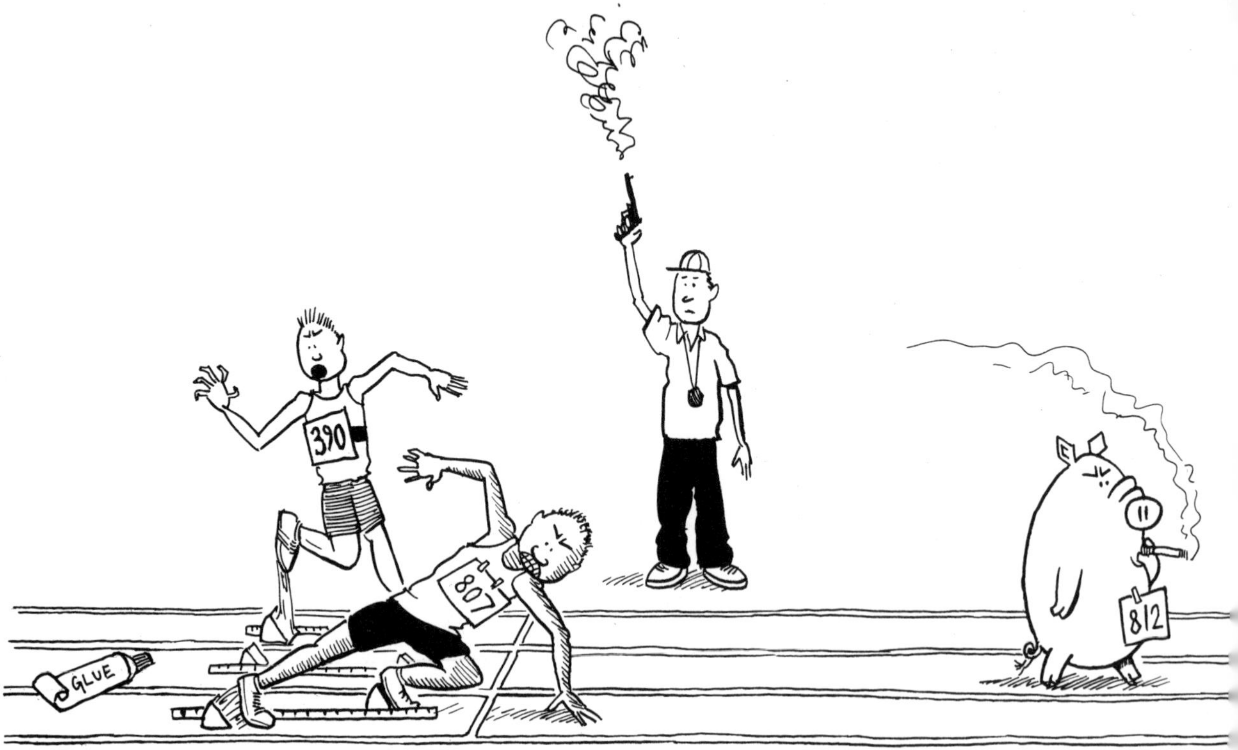

390
807
GLUE
812

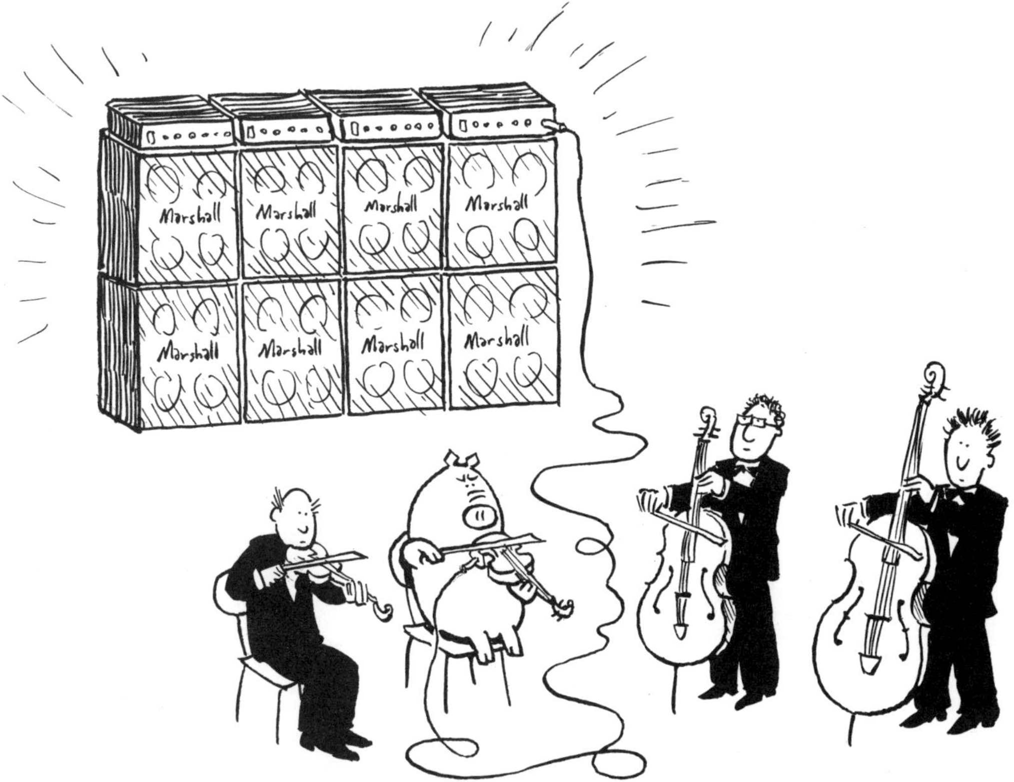
Marshall
Marshall
Marshall
Marshall
Marshall
Marshall
Marshall
Marshall

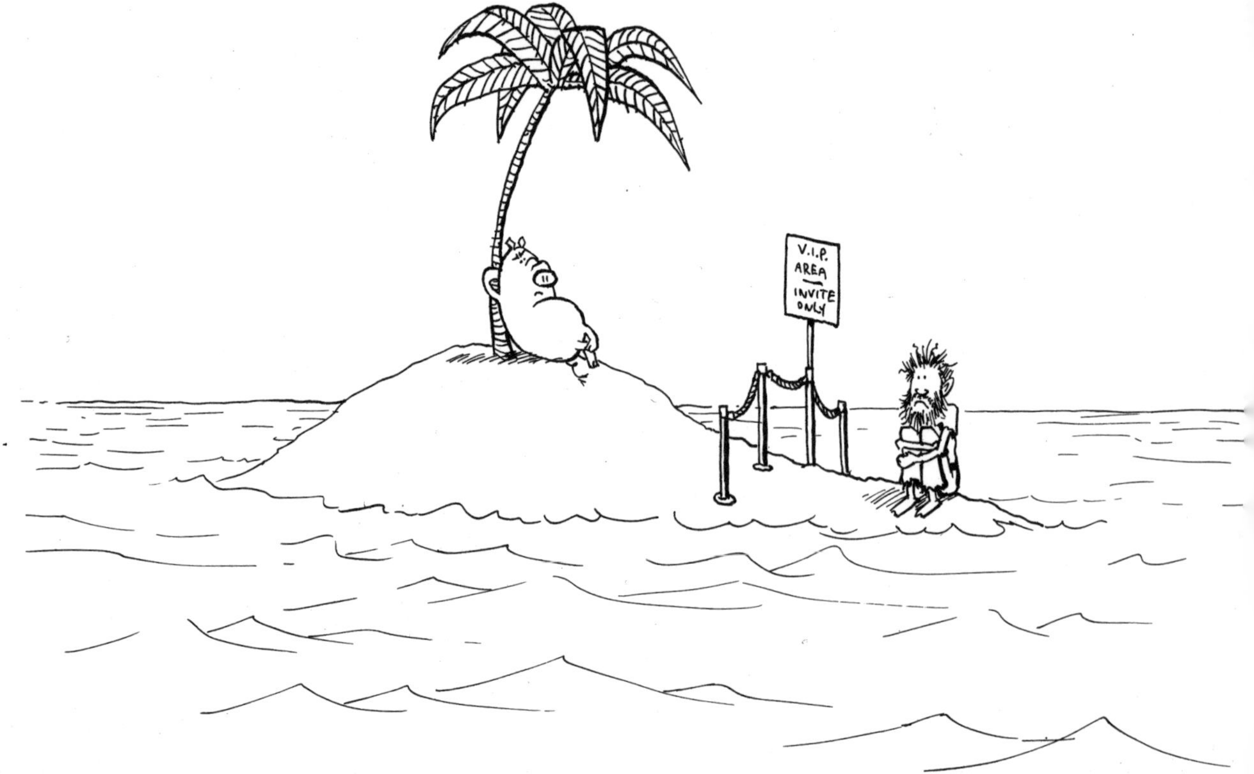
V.I.P.
AREA
INVITE
ONLY

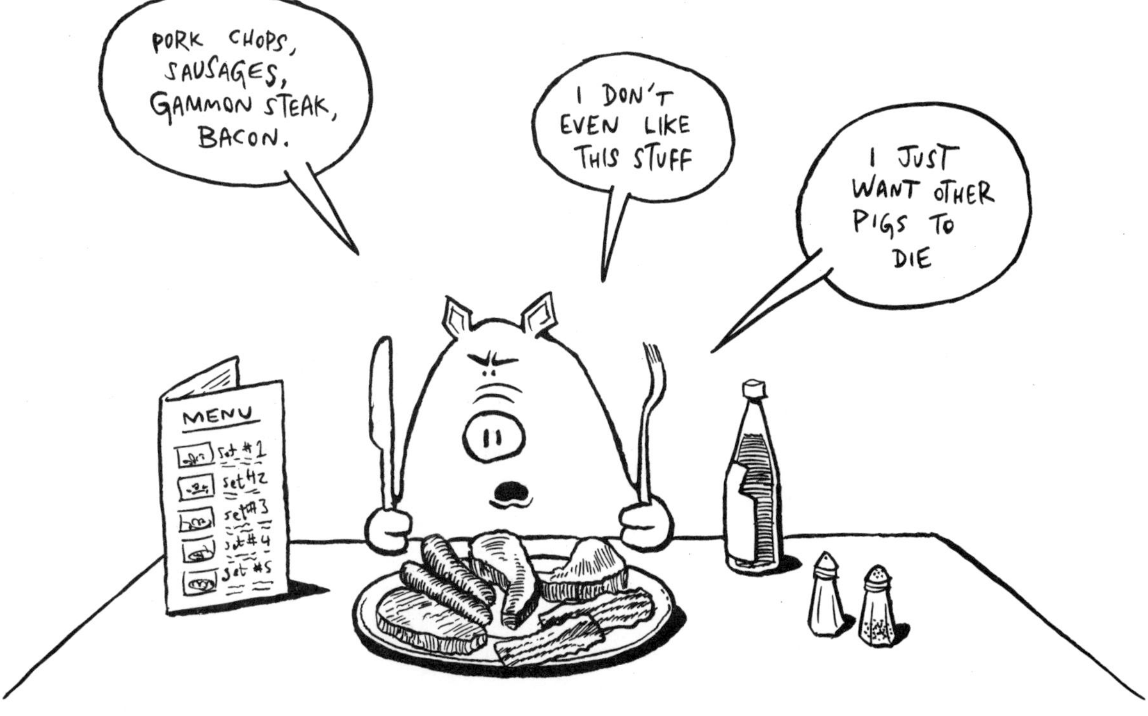
PORK CHOPS, SAUSAGES, GAMMON STEAK, BACON.
I DON'T EVEN LIKE THIS STUFF
I JUST WANT OTHER PIGS TO DIE
MENU
Set #1
set #2
set #3
set #4
Set #5

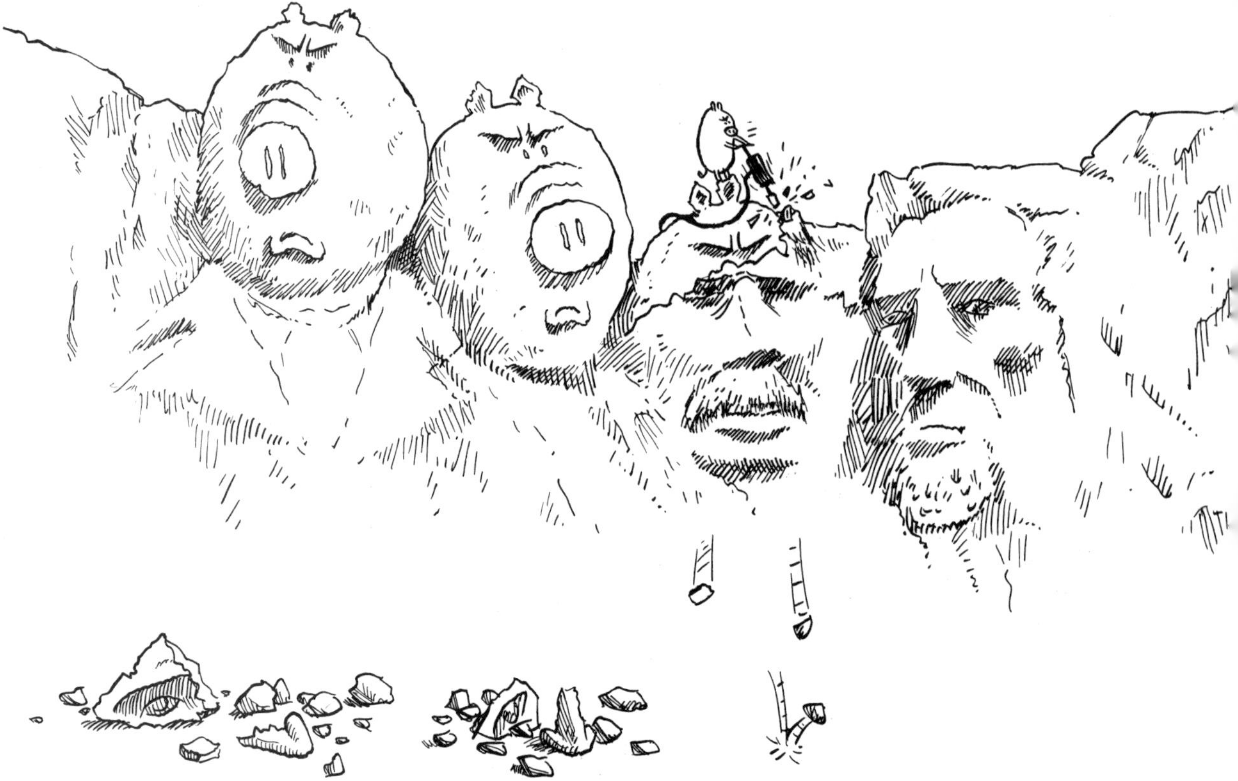

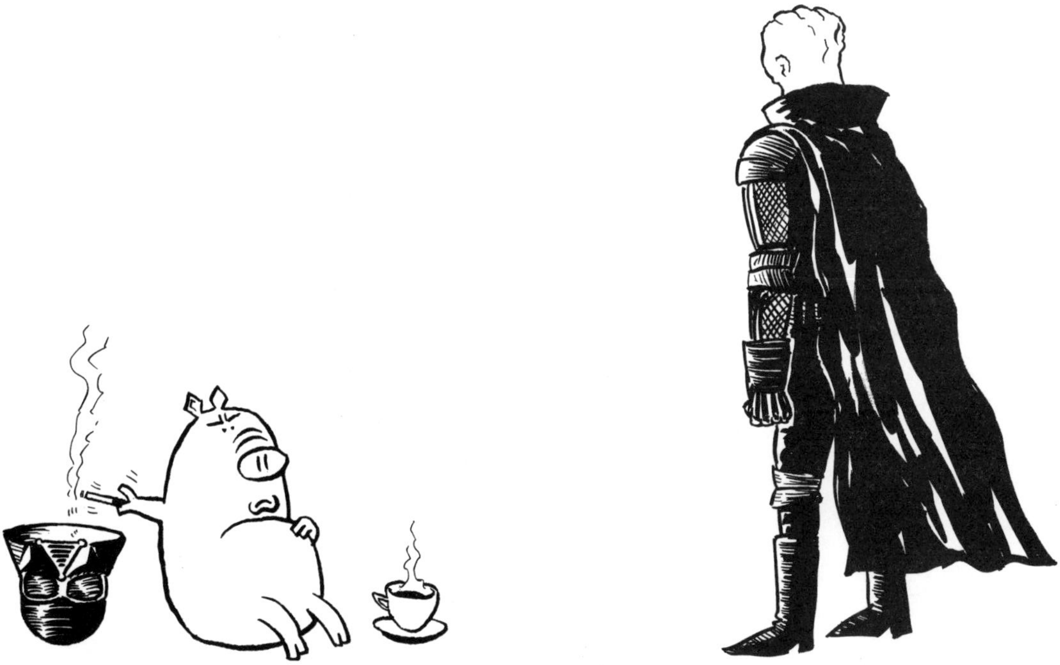

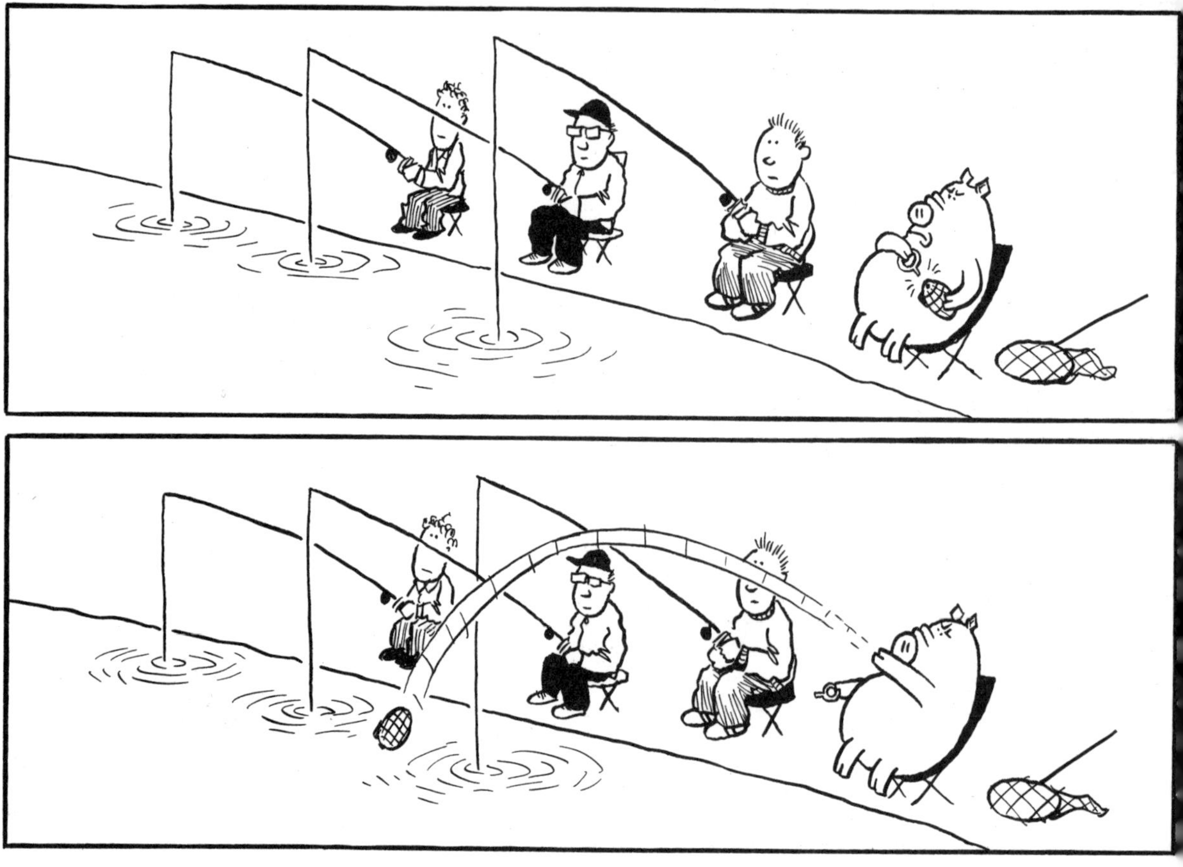

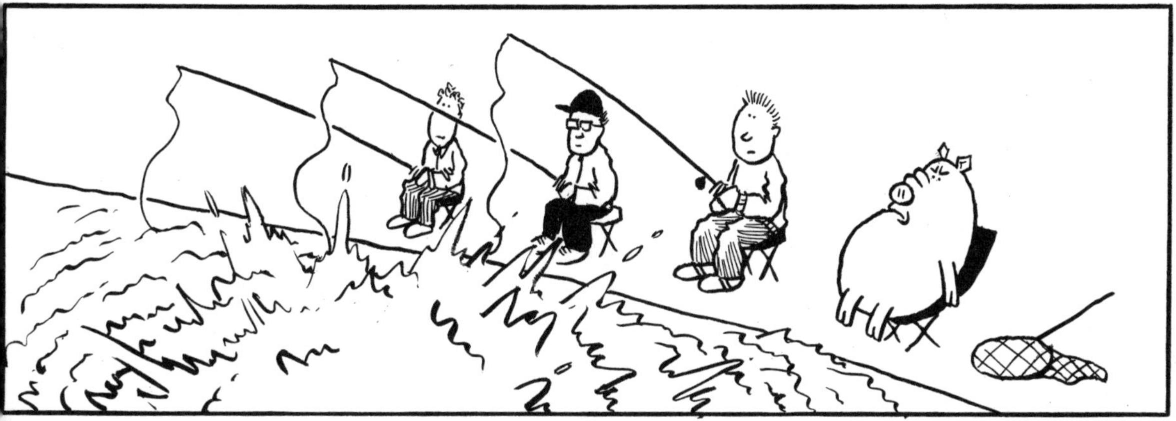

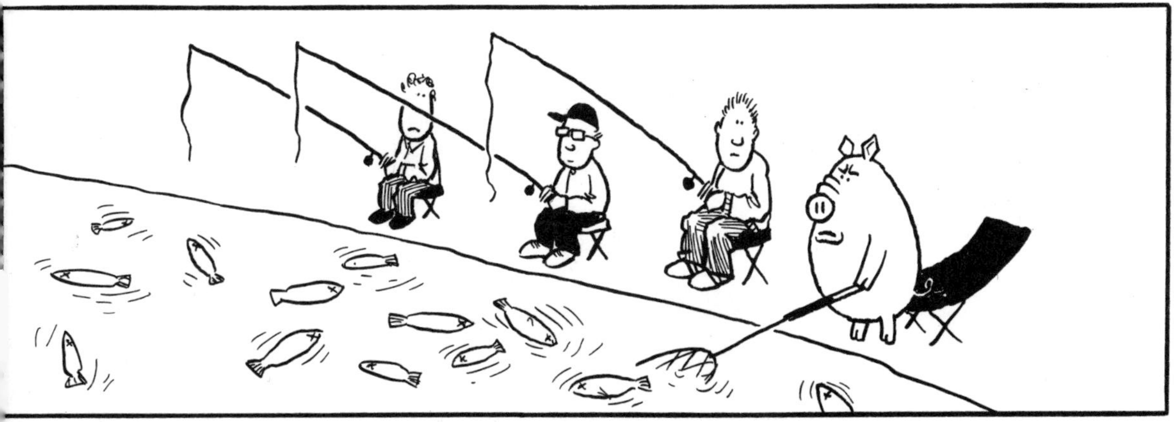

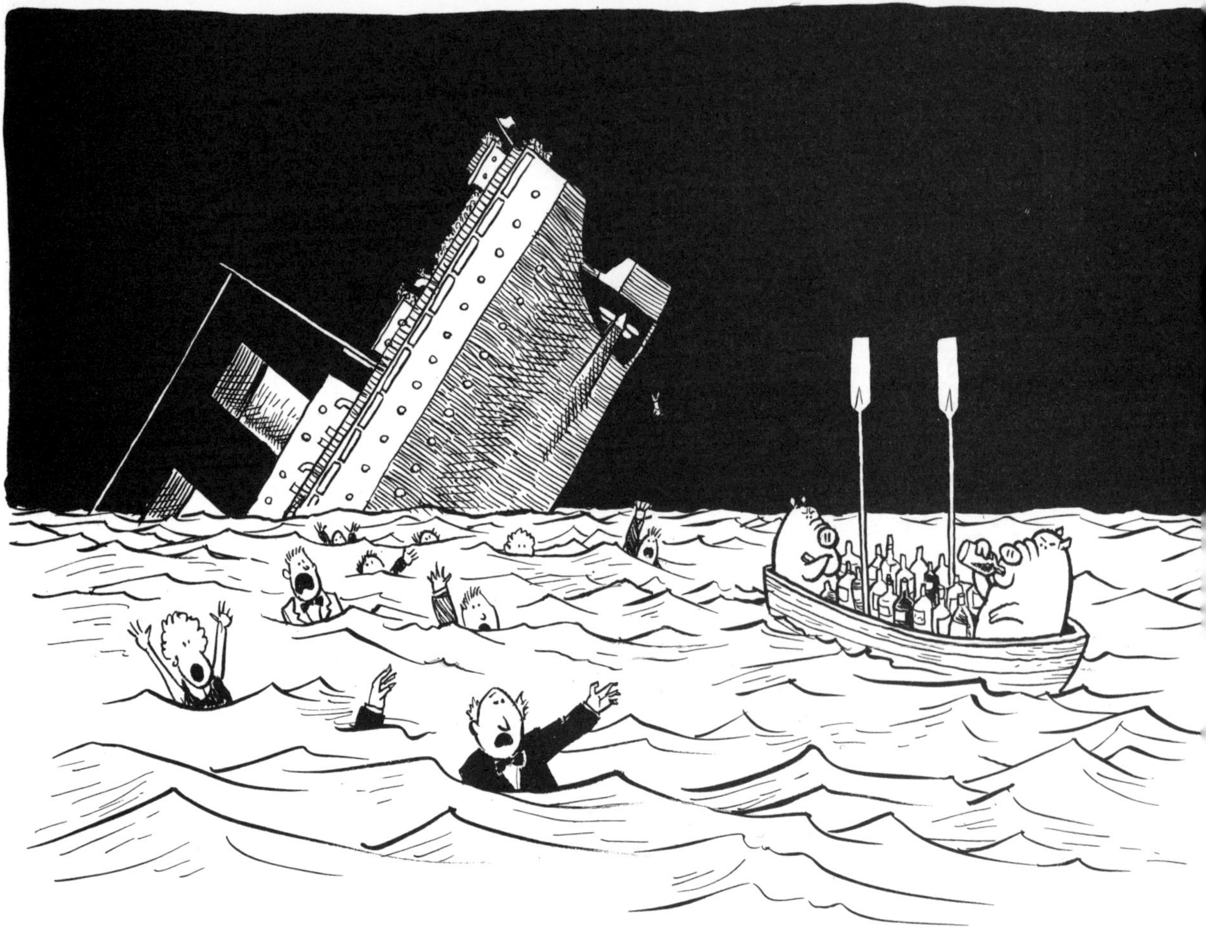

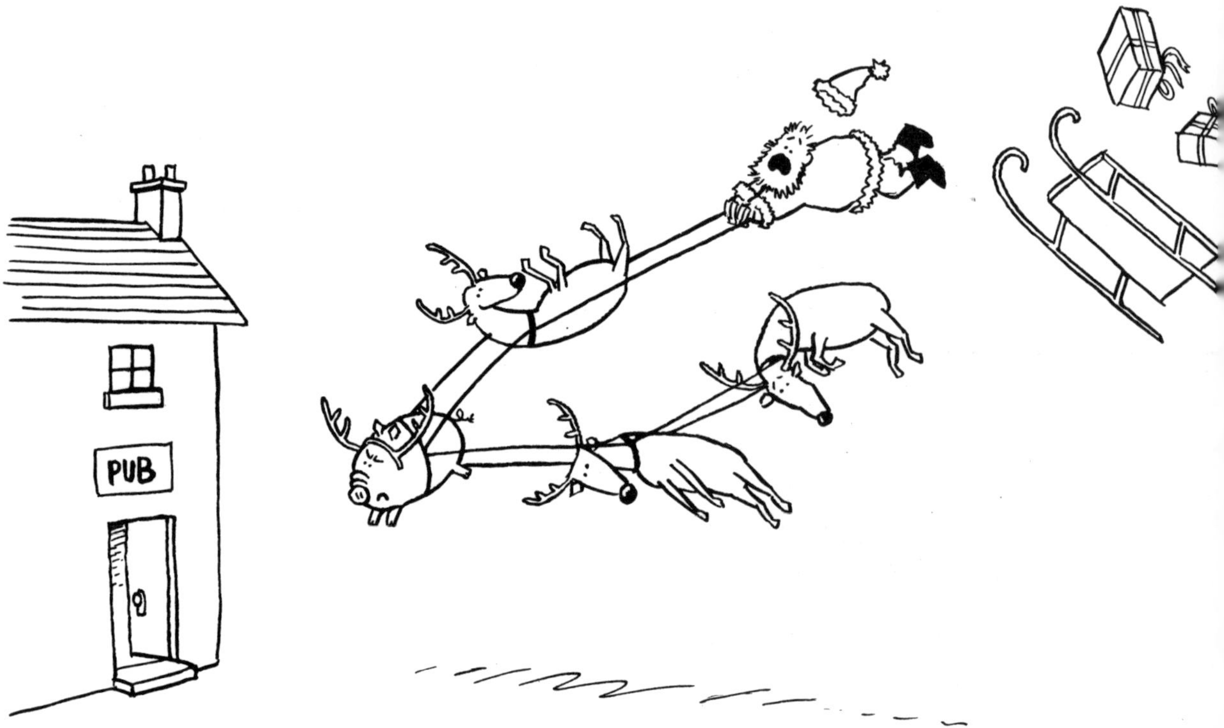
PUB

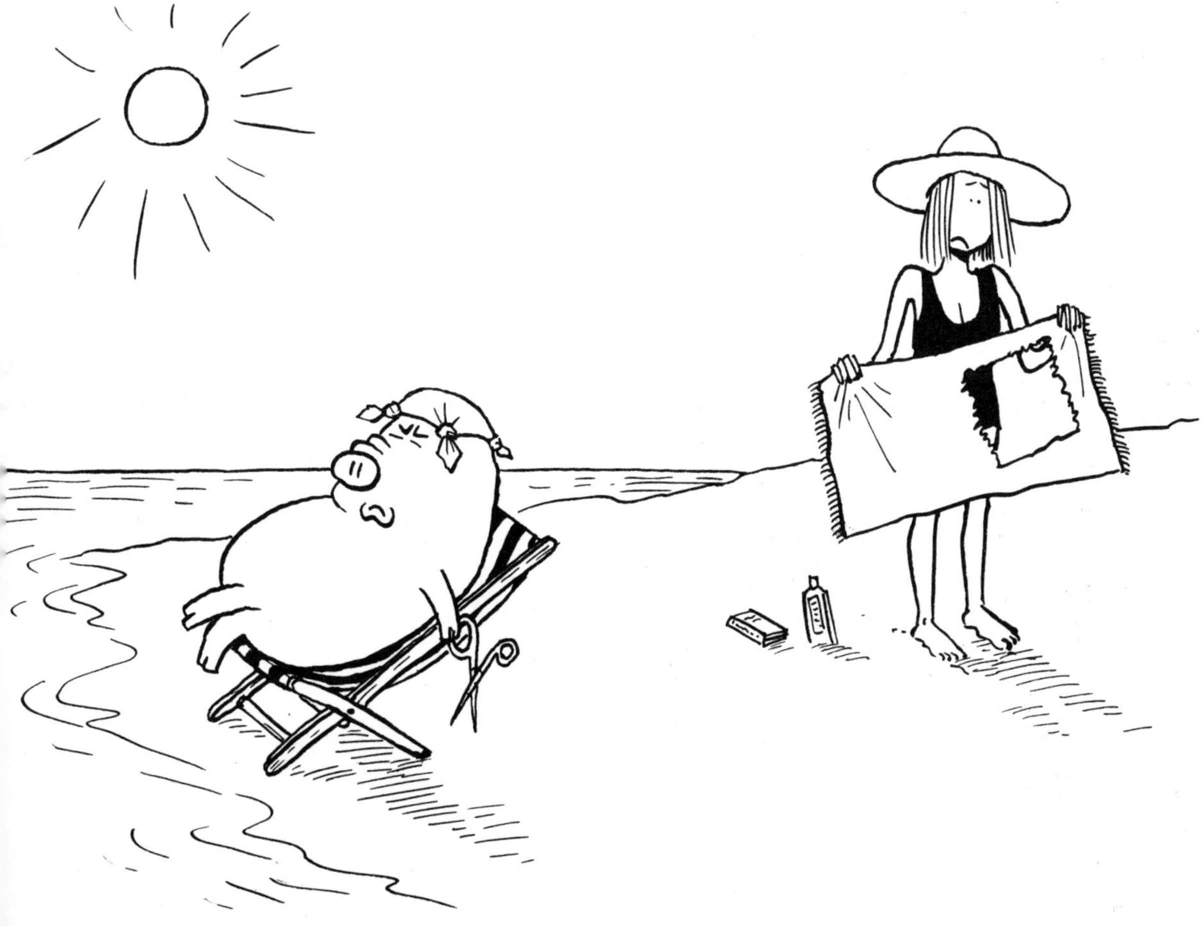

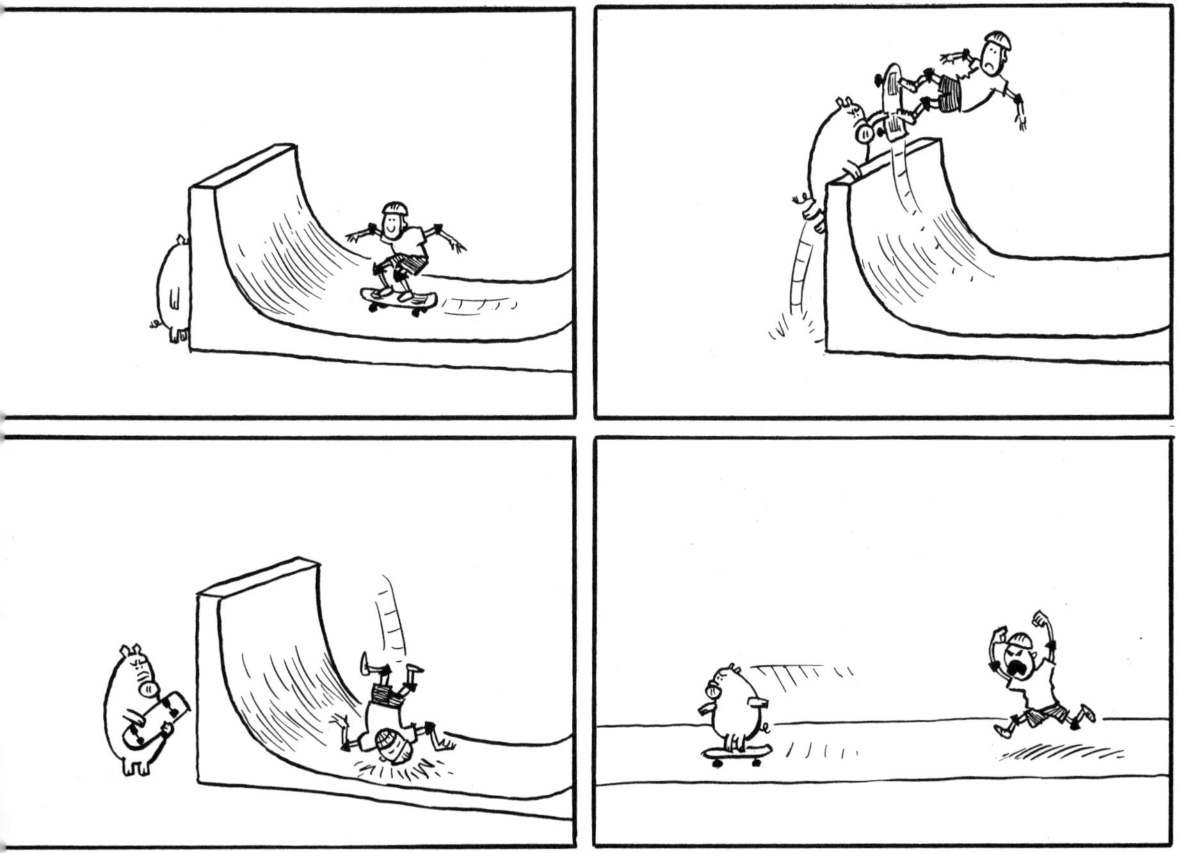

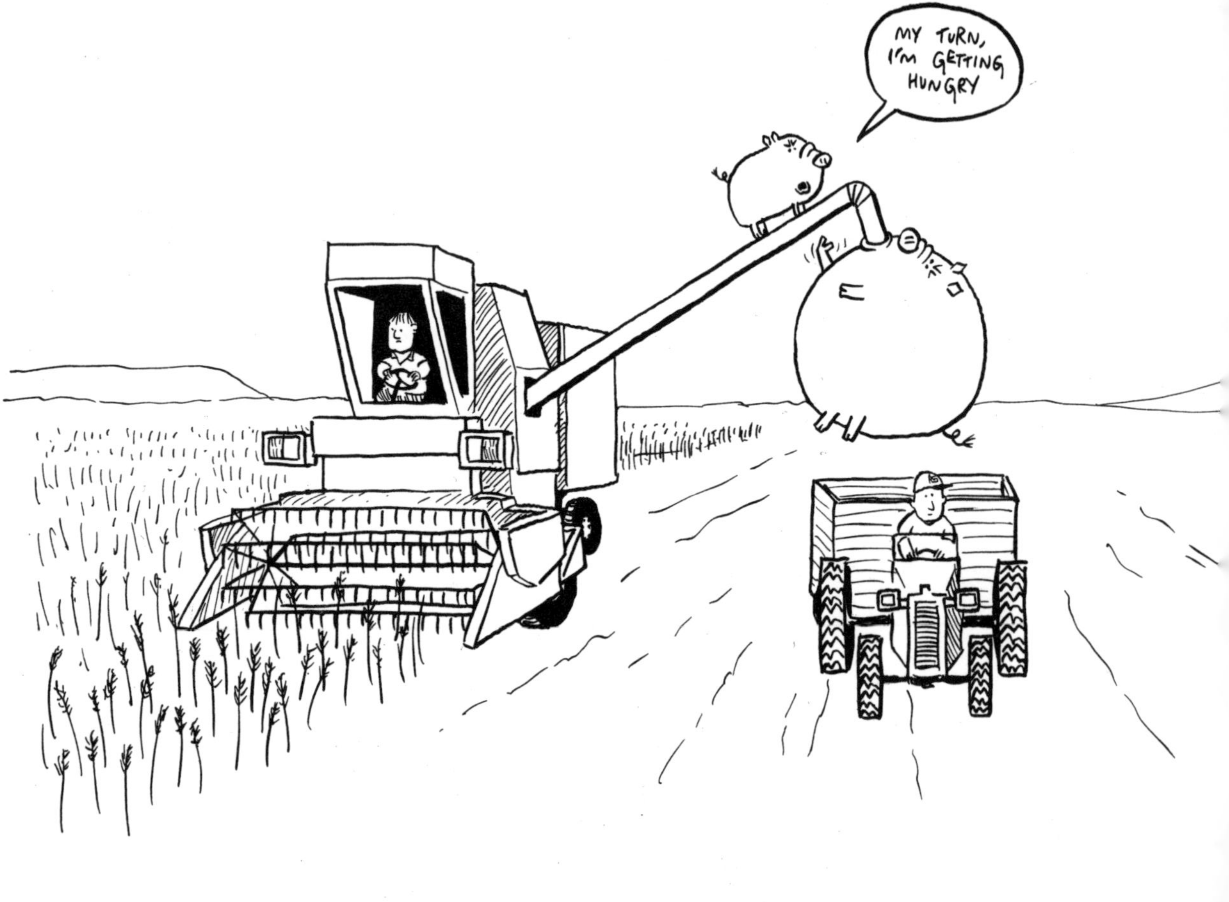
MY TURN, I'M GETTING HUNGRY

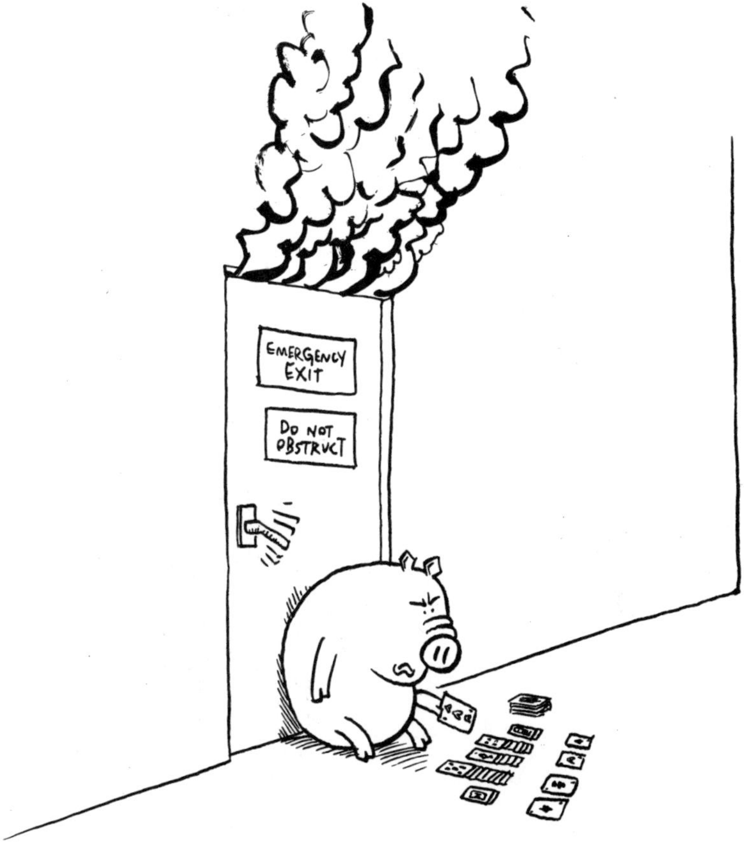
EMERGENCY EXIT
DO NOT OBSTRUCT

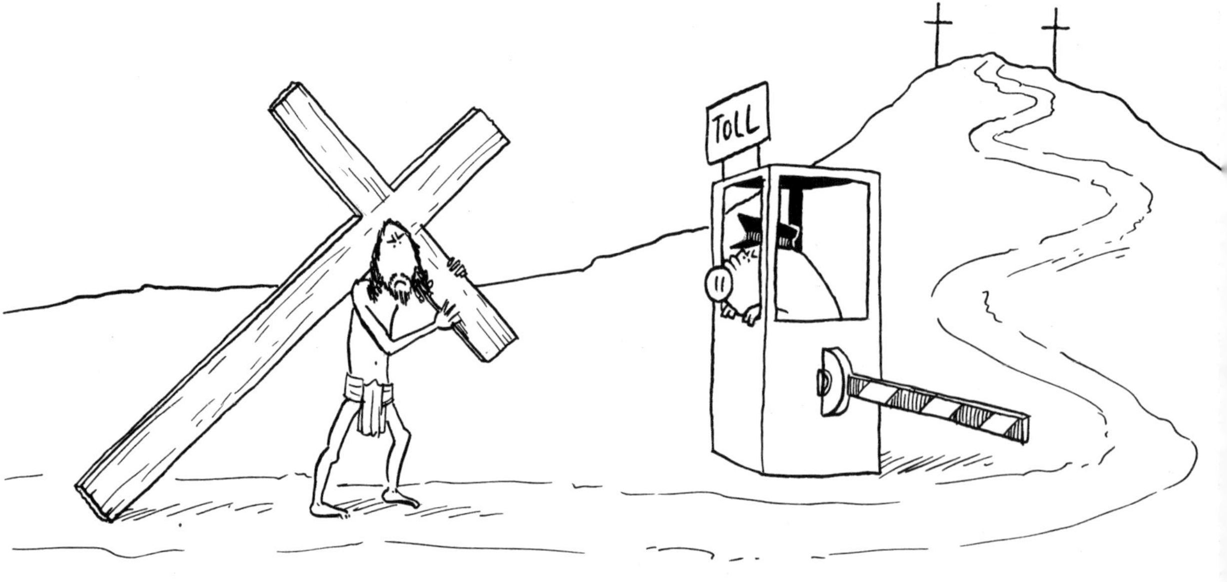
TOLL

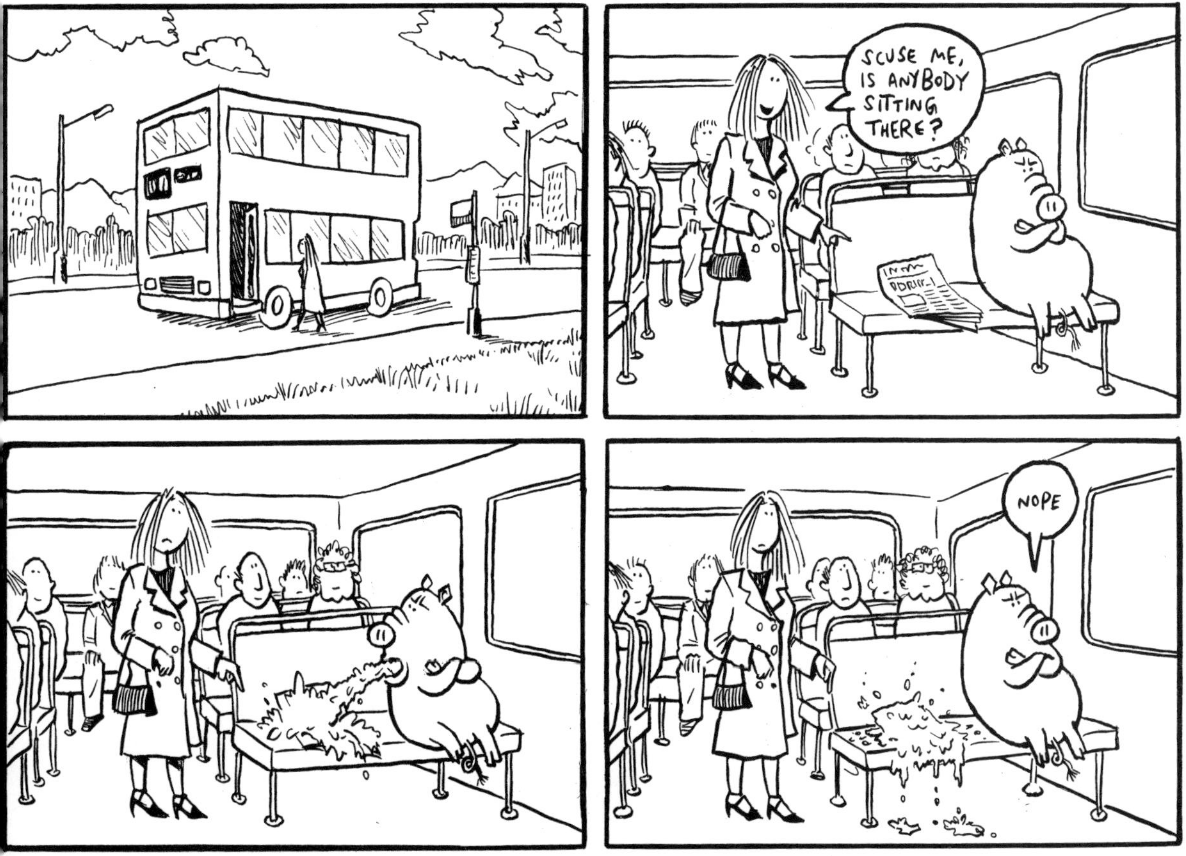
SCUSE ME, IS ANYBODY SITTING THERE?
NOPE

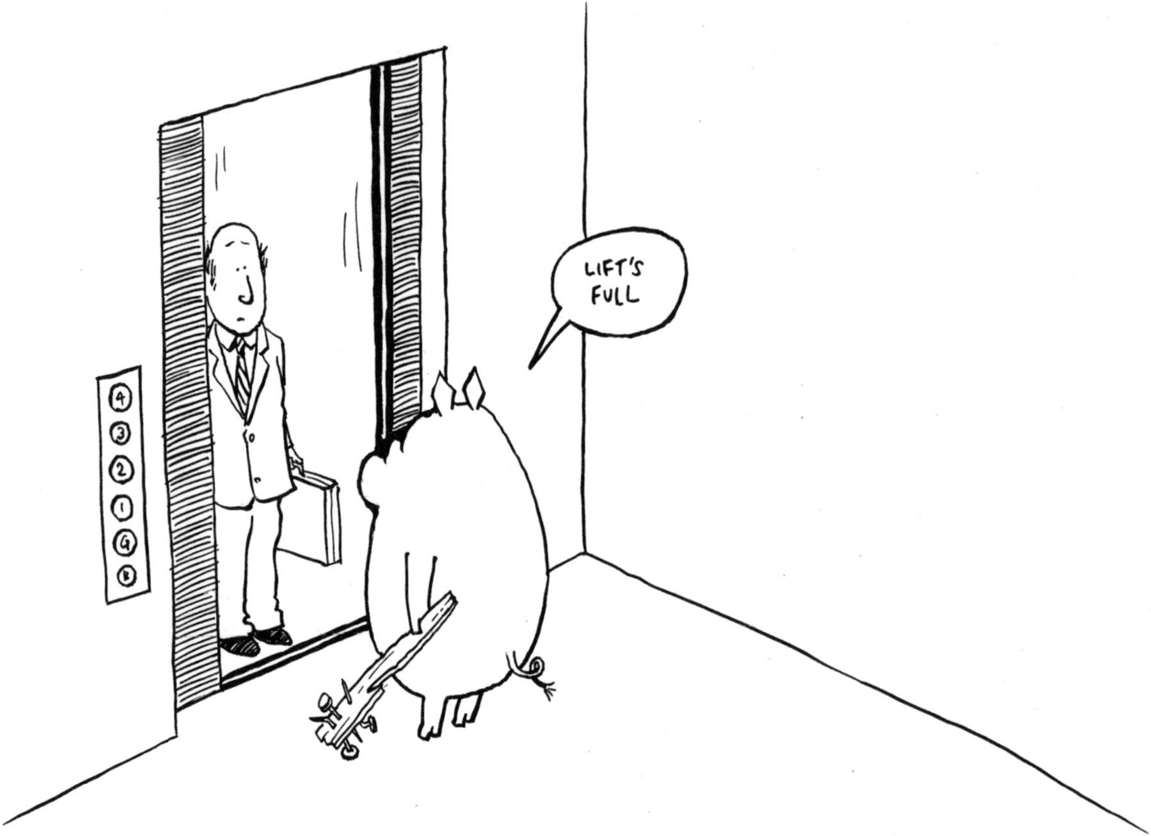
4
3
2
1
G
B
LIFT'S FULL

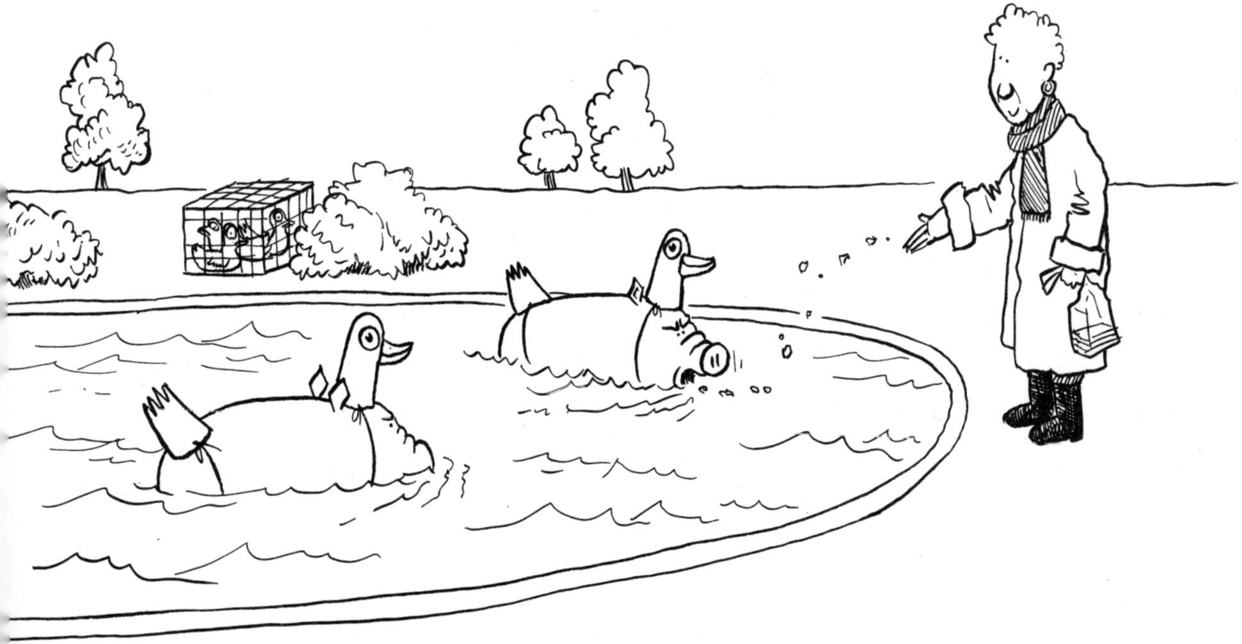

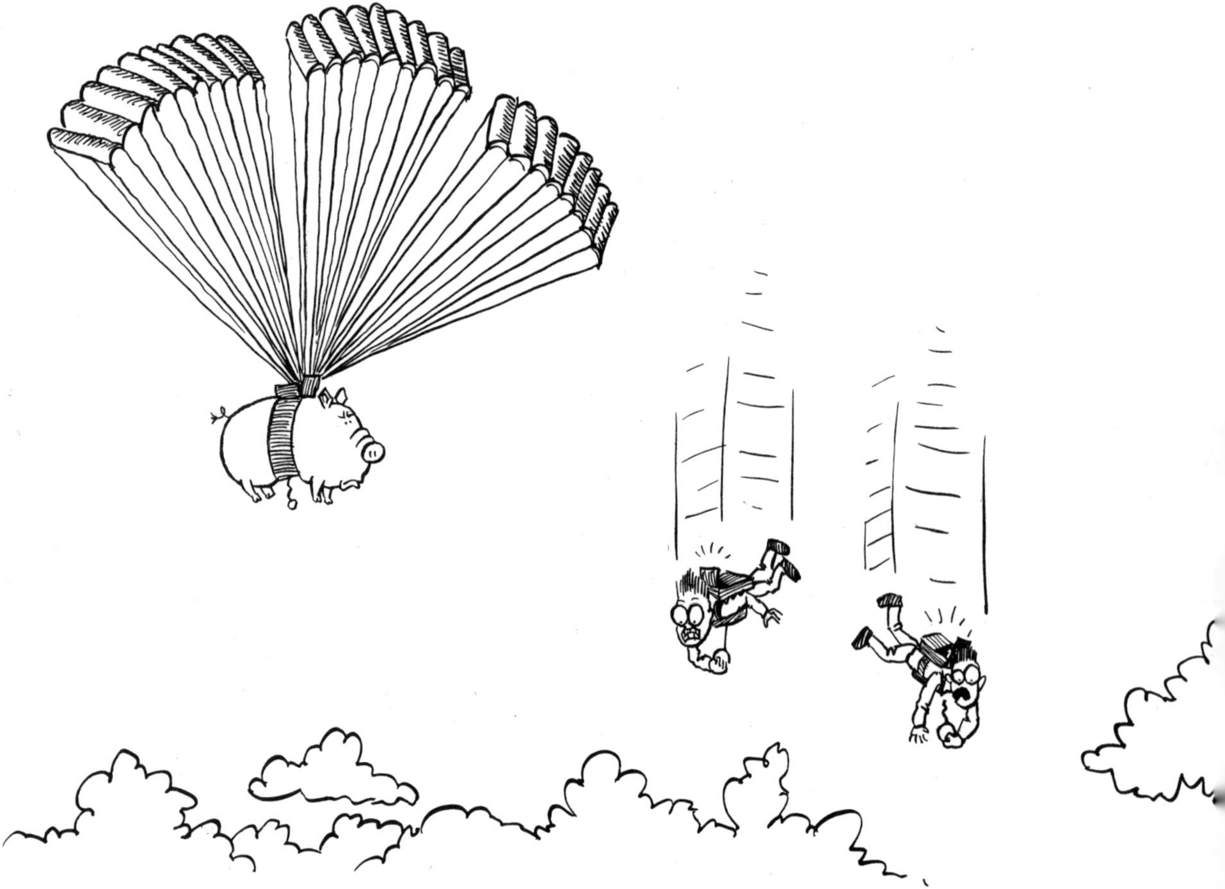

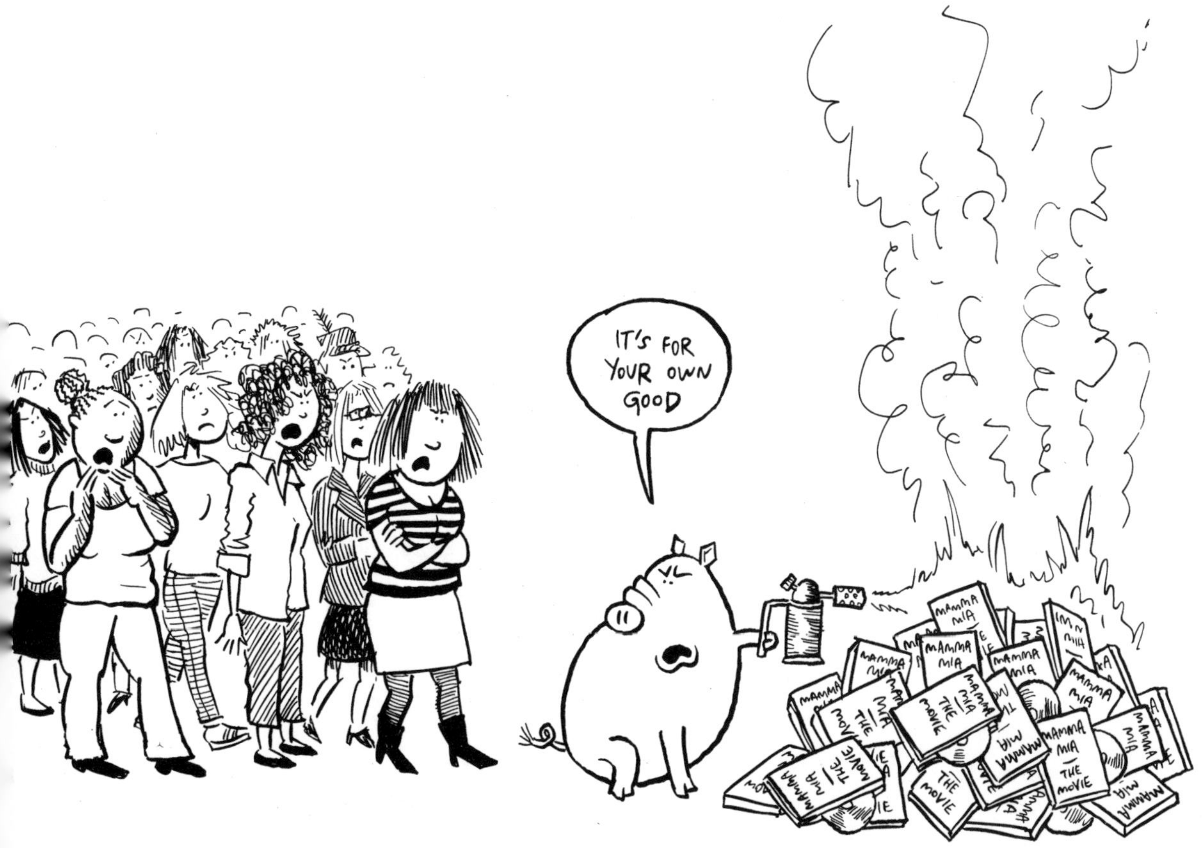
IT'S FOR YOUR OWN GOOD
MAMMA MIA — THE MOVIE

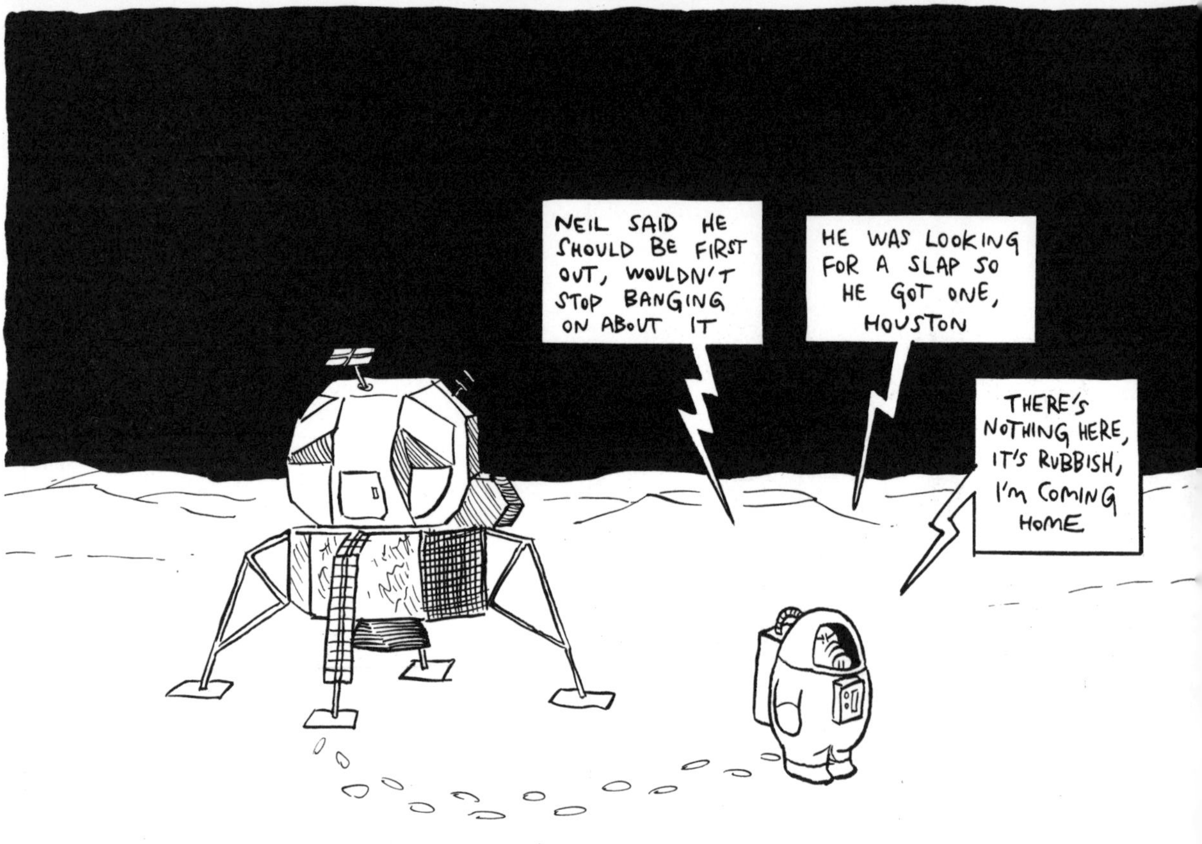
NEIL SAID HE SHOULD BE FIRST OUT, WOULDN'T STOP BANGING ON ABOUT IT
HE WAS LOOKING FOR A SLAP SO HE GOT ONE, HOUSTON
THERE'S NOTHING HERE, IT'S RUBBISH, I'M COMING HOME

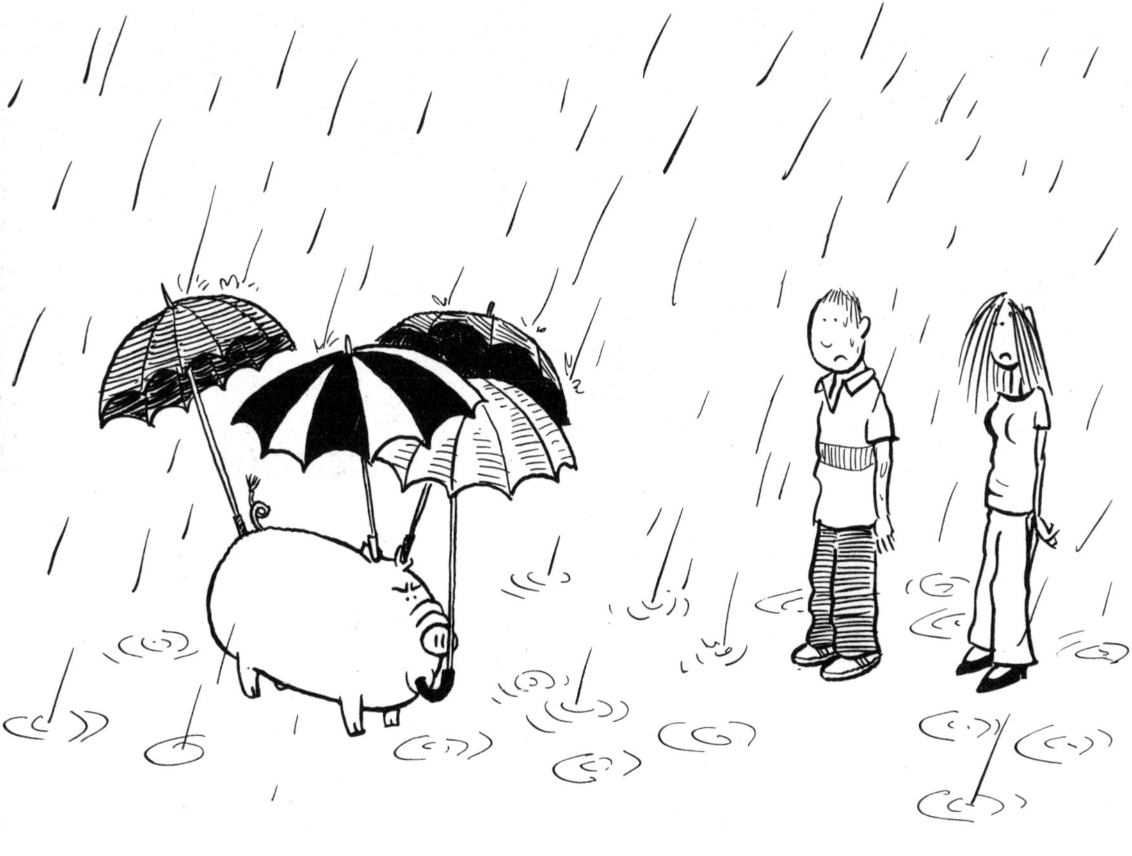

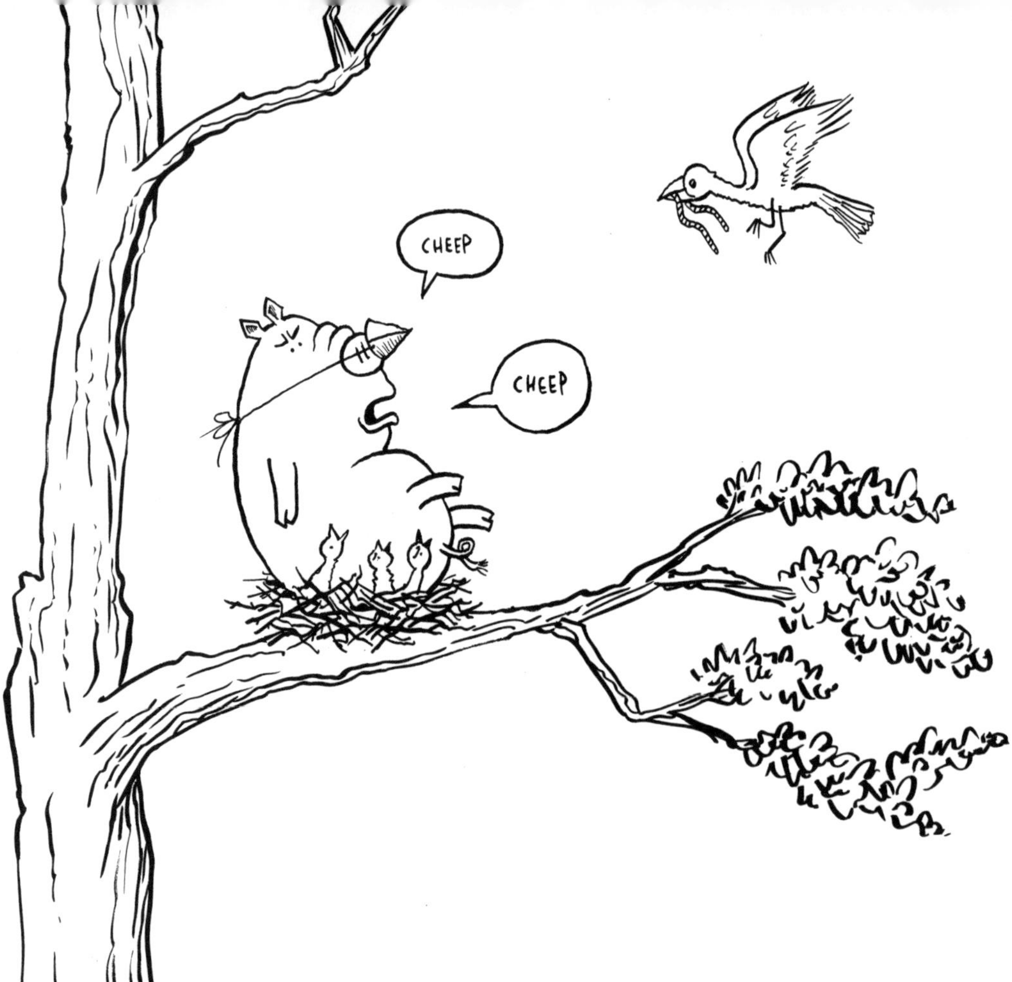
CHEEP
CHEEP

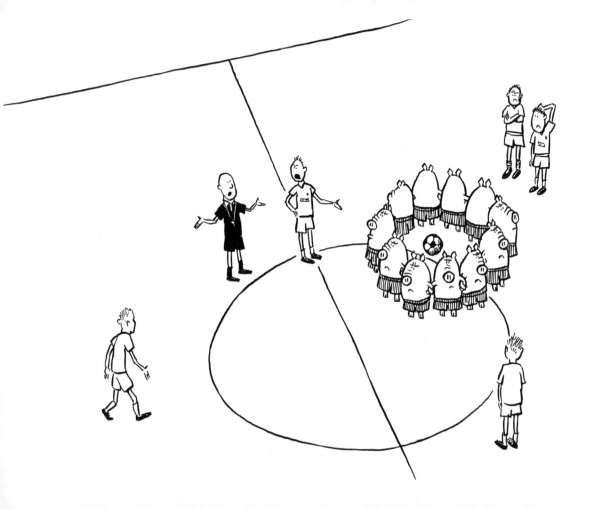

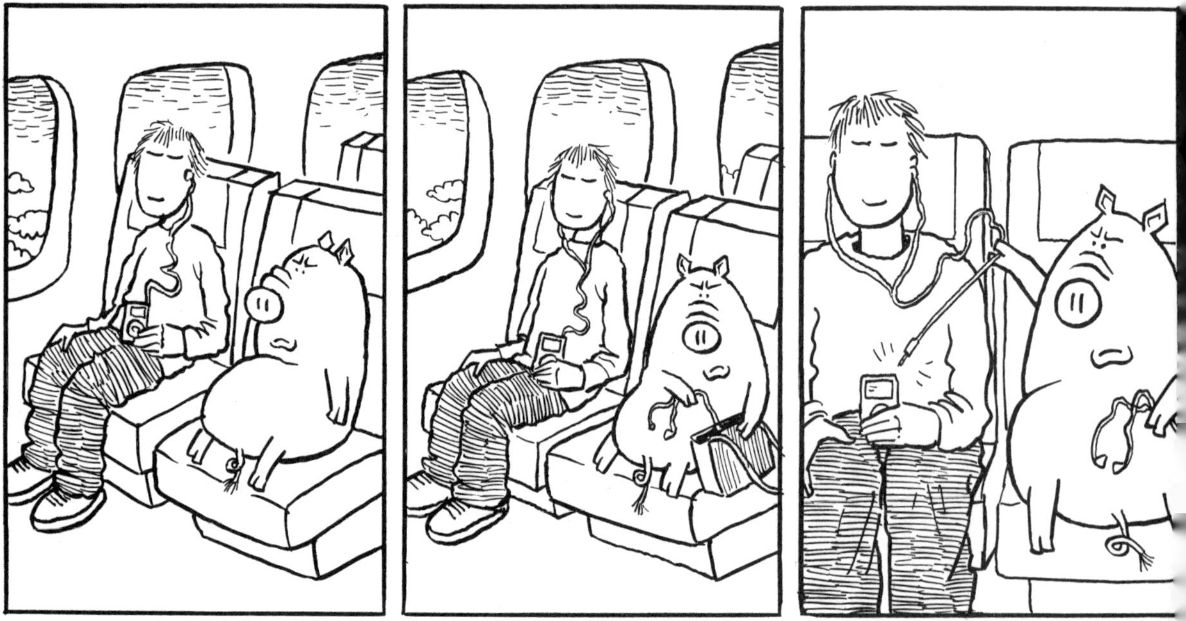

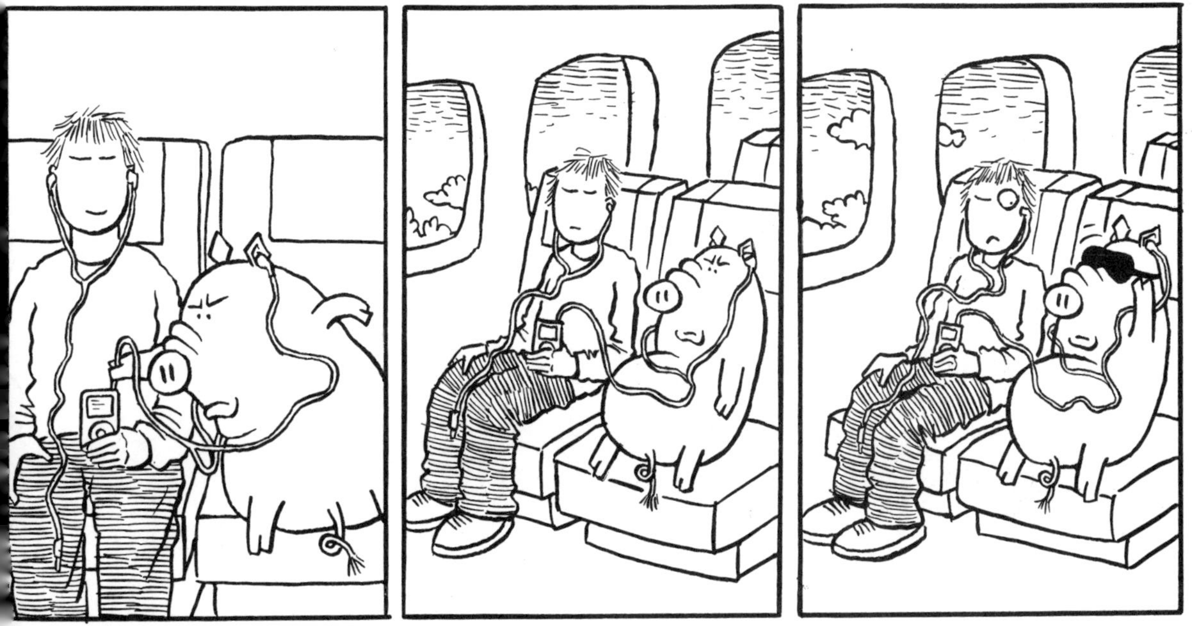

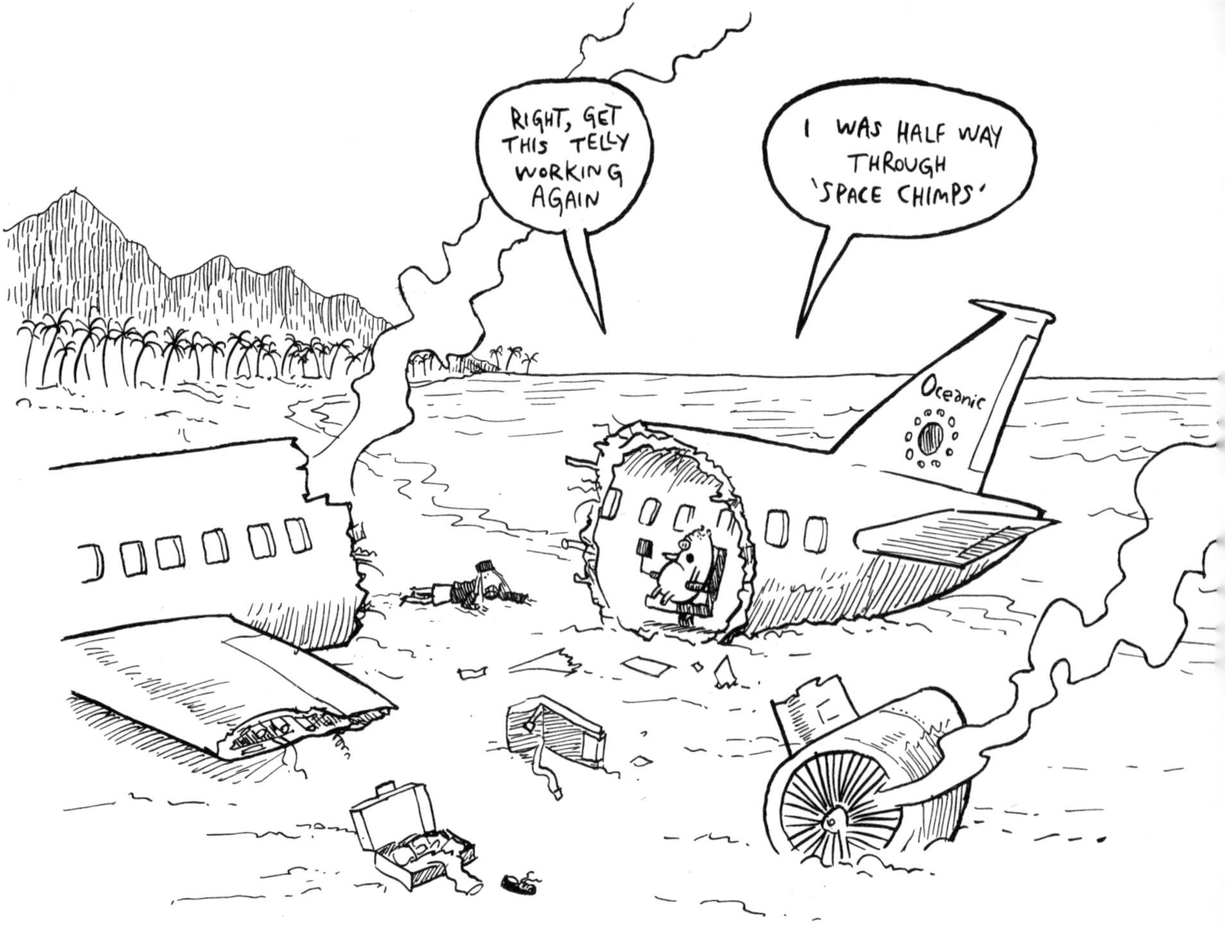
RIGHT, GET THIS TELLY WORKING AGAIN
I WAS HALF WAY THROUGH 'SPACE CHIMPS'
Oceanic

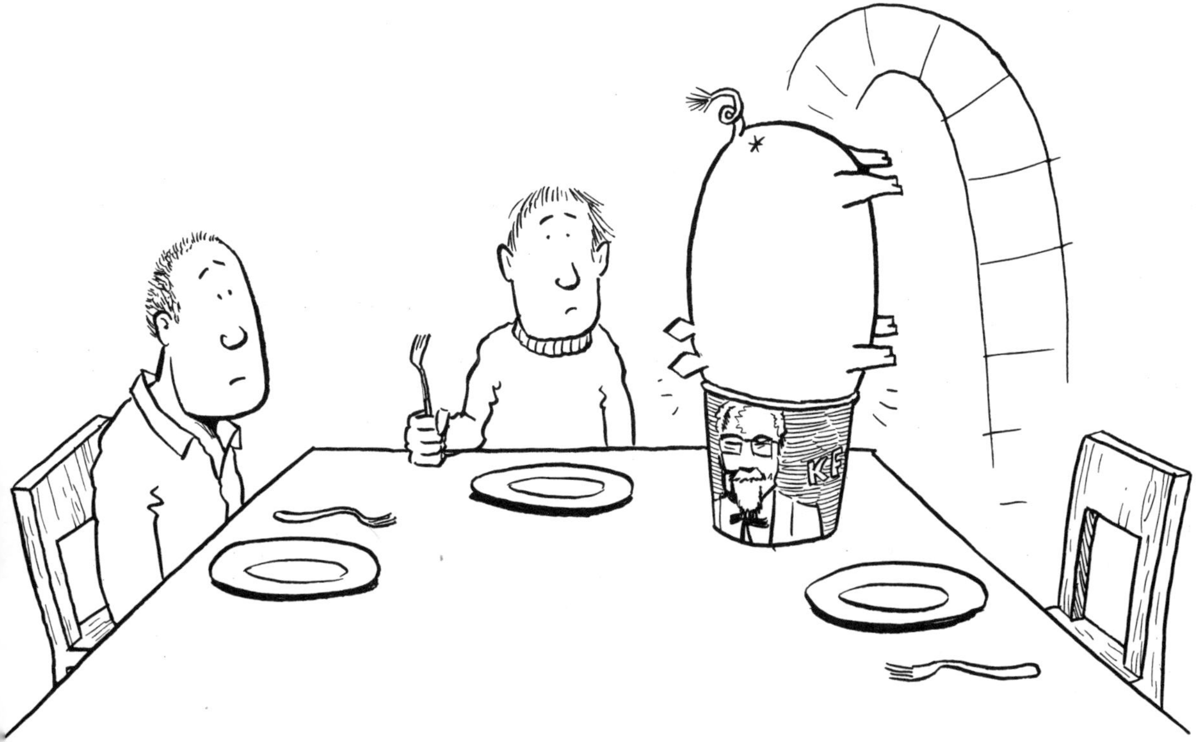
KF

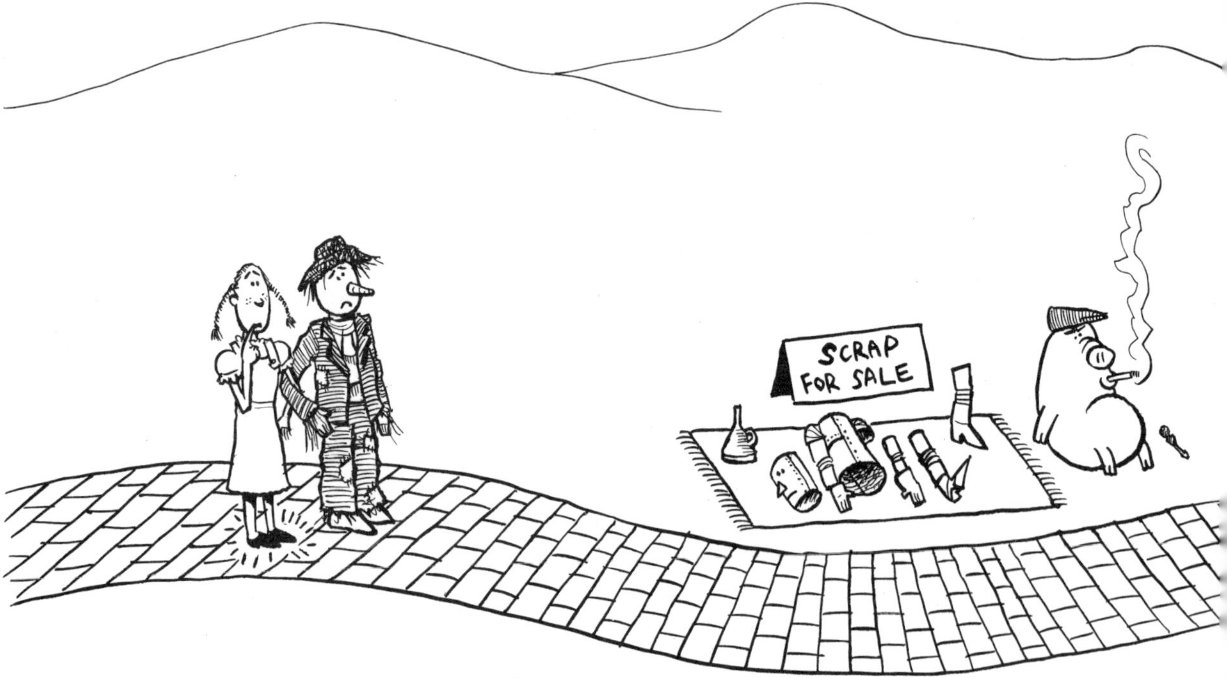
SCRAP
FOR SALE

CAUSE YOU WERE BEING BORING

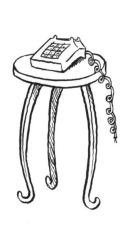

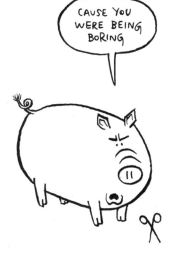

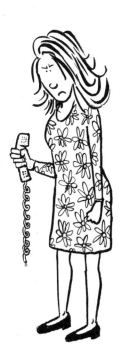

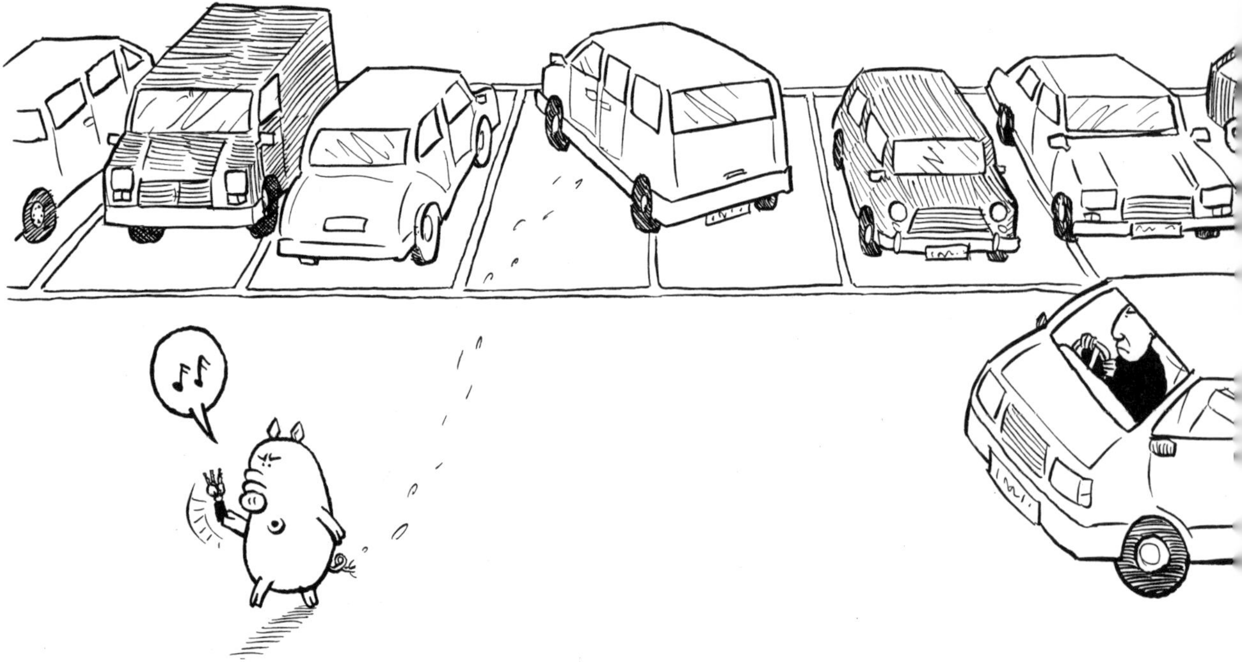

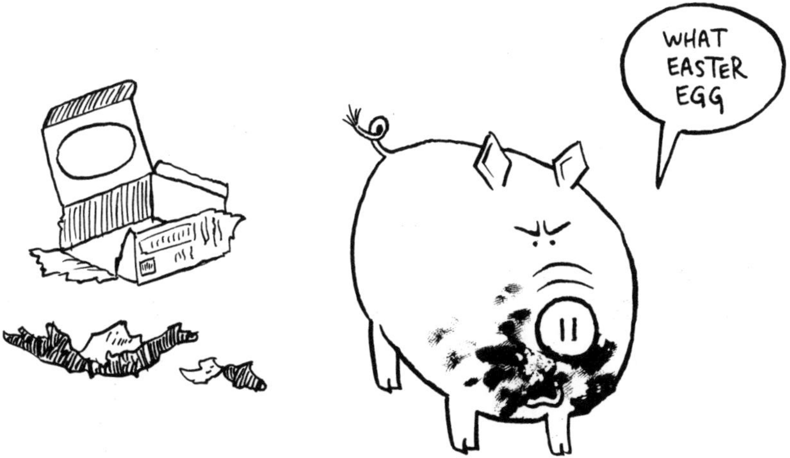
WHAT EASTER EGG

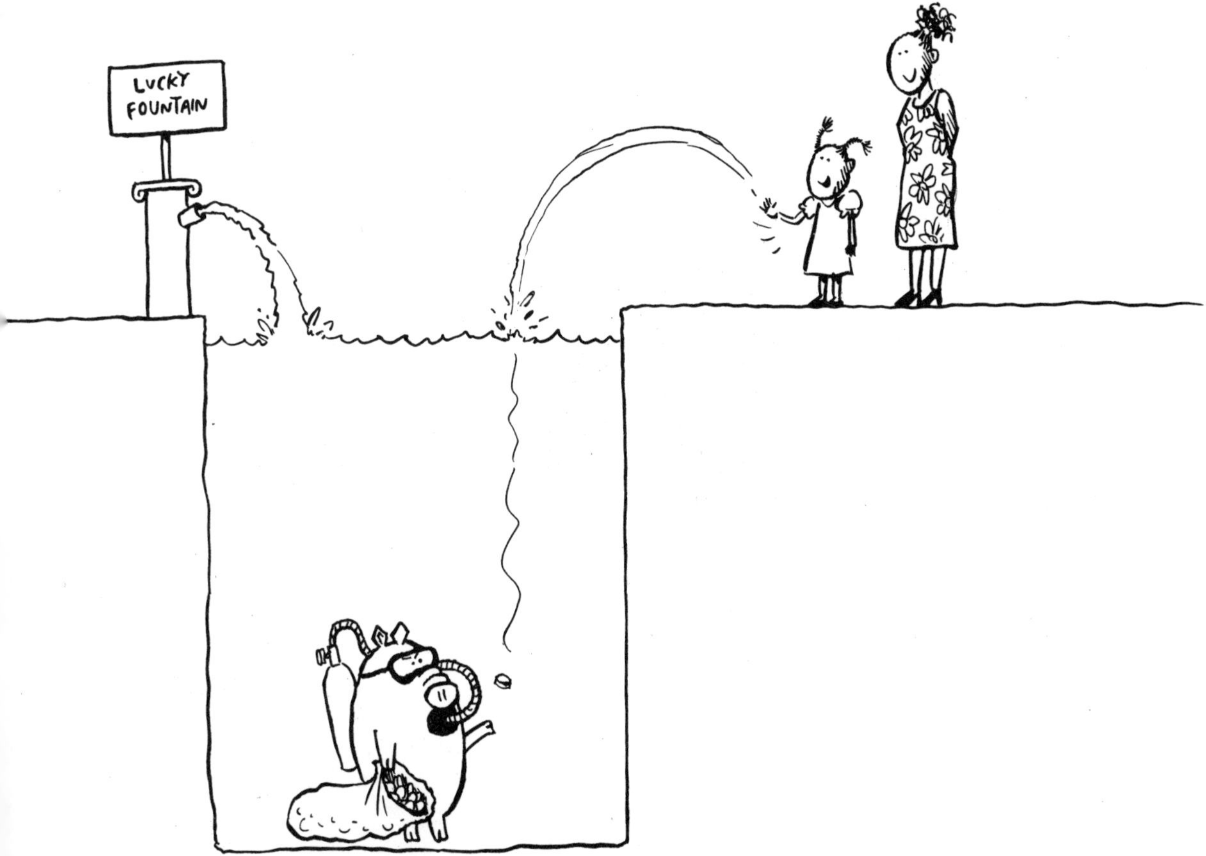
LUCKY
FOUNTAIN

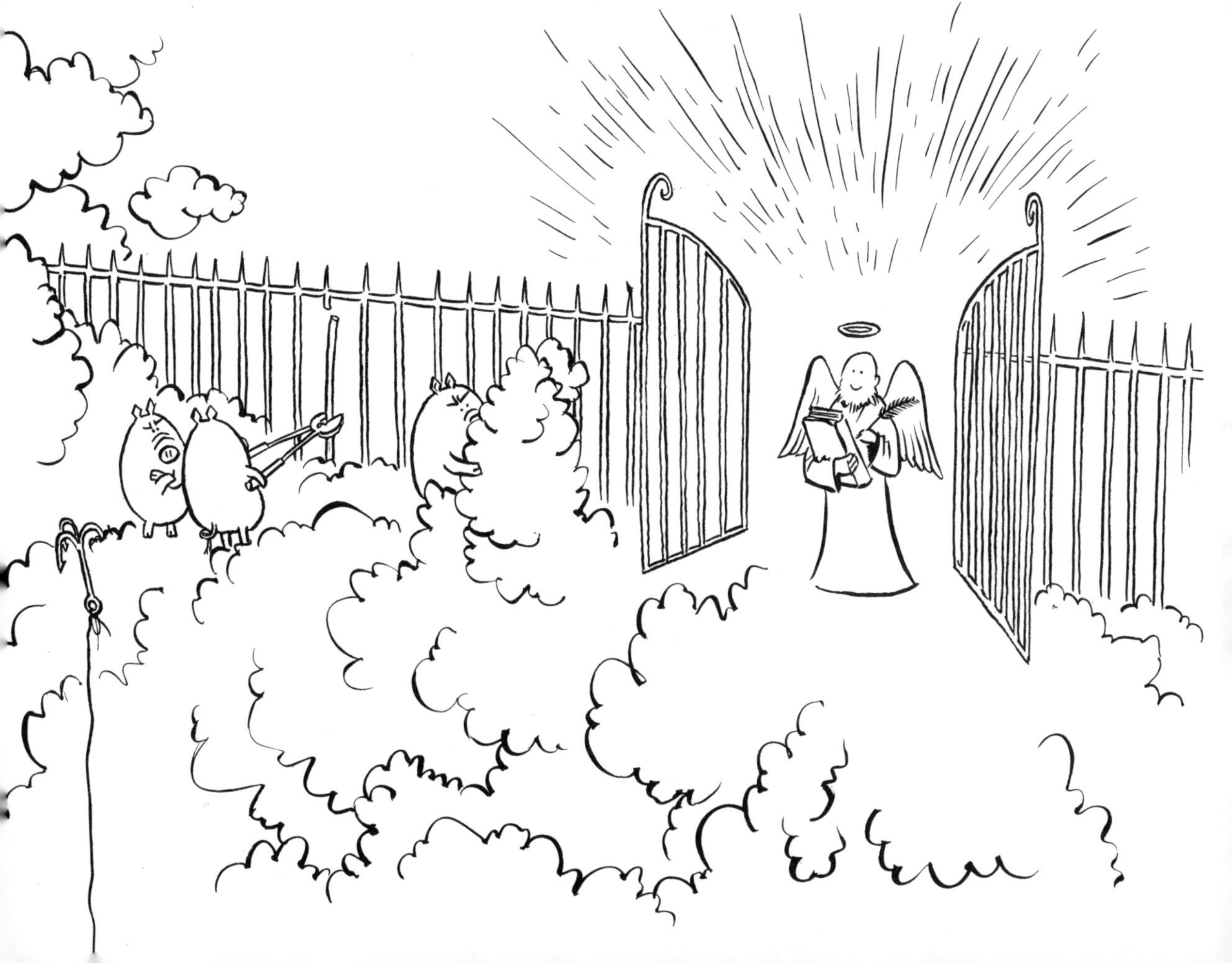

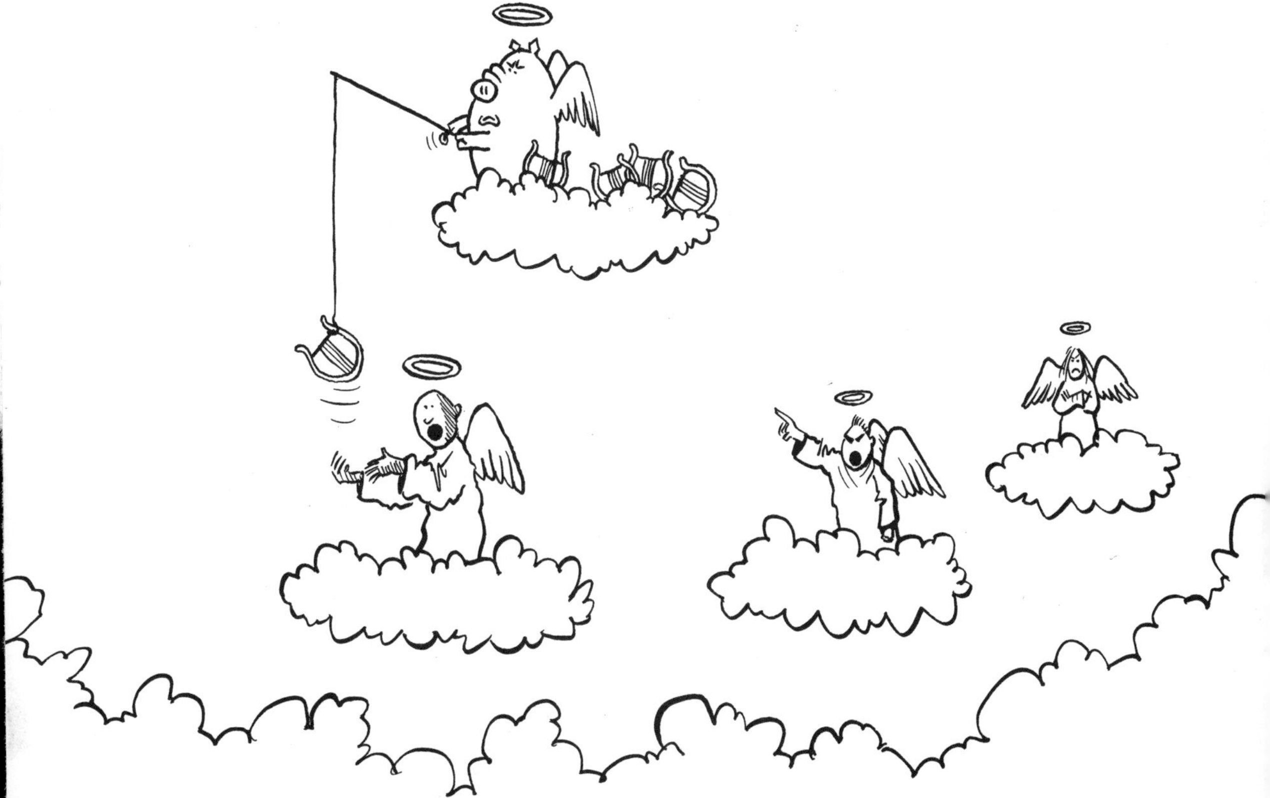

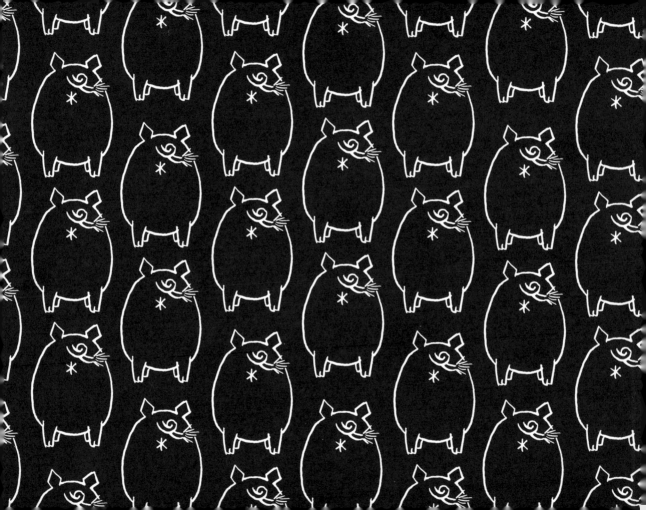